Mary Lily Walker:
Forgotten Visionary of Dundee

Eddie Small

Dundee University Press

First published in Great Britain in 2013
by Dundee University Press
University of Dundee DD1 4HN
www.dundee.ac.uk/dup

ISBN: 9781845861636

With thanks to the University of Dundee Archives

British Library Cataloguing-in-Publication Data
A catalogue record for this book is available
on request from the British Library

Designed by Brett Housego
Typeset in Garamond Premier Pro

Cover illustration by Julie Reilly

Printed and Bound in Great Britain by
TJ International Ltd, Padstow

MIX
Paper from
responsible sources
FSC® C013056

Contents

A Dedication to the Memory of Myra Baillie

Myra Baillie came to Dundee from Canada's McMasters University in 1996 to undertake and complete a thesis on Mary Lily Walker, and in so doing revived wonderful memories of a Dundee heroine that had all but vanished. During her stay, Myra became a regular and welcomed visitor to most of the archives and libraries in Dundee and St Andrews, and the depth of knowledge she accrued was astounding.

In 2004 Myra completed a PhD thesis entitled *Women in the Munitions Factories in Glasgow*, which won her the prize for the best doctoral thesis in Canada that year. Her supervisor remembers her as being *'intelligent, kind, thoughtful and of splendid character'*.

The striking similarities in nature and intellect between Mary Lily and Myra are easily found.

Without Myra this book could not have been contemplated.

Myra Baillie passed away on 11th May 2005. She was 57 years of age.

Acknowledgements

Writing this book, and on such a worthwhile subject, was a privilege, and I owe a debt of gratitude to several nice people. My first *'thank you'* goes to Anna Day, of Dundee University Press, for inviting me to write the story of Mary Lily Walker. Not a dry history – bring her to life! That was her total instruction. At the other end of the work, I bow to my proof-reading and support team of Lee Fairlie, and her mother Joyce, who worked late and long, and put up with much.

Each of the four people who visited the grave of Mary Lily with me in August 2012 played a great part in producing this book, and I name them in alphabetical order.

David Dobson's research work was priceless, whilst his quiet support was gladly received. He, in turn, would like to give thanks to the staff at each of the following establishments: National Archives of Scotland, The Special Collections of St Andrews University Library, The Mitchell Library in Glasgow, Dundee University Archives, Dundee City Archives, Wellgate Library in Dundee, St Paul's Cathedral in Dundee, Tay Valley Family History Society.

Brett Housego kept a smile on all our faces, and his expertise with camera and computer was inspiring. Again, Brett was utterly supportive throughout.

Pete Kinnear is a very tall man with a prodigious appetite for work. His meticulous research has underpinned so much of this book, and his opinion has solved many of its puzzles.

Whilst I extend my sincere thanks to Pete, he would like to mention those who especially aided him: Maia Sheridan, Muira Mackenzie, Catriona Foote and Briony Aitchison at St Andrews University Archives, Special Collections; Eileen Moran, Maureen Reid, Carol Smith, Deirdre Sweeney and Kerrin Evans at Central Library Dundee, Local History Section; Dundee University Archives – all the staff were very helpful, but particular thanks to Kenneth Baxter and Michael Bolik; Ian Flett and the staff at Dundee City Archives; staff at National Library of Scotland, Edinburgh, and Keith Walker.

Suzanne Zeedyk has driven much of the entire project. Her enthusiasm was boundless, her energy limitless, and her powers of persuasion impressive. Her intuition has been uncanny – well, almost all of the time. It has been a great pleasure to be involved with Suzanne, who also has some people she especially wants to mention: *'I would like to thank Chris Whatley, Charles McKean, and Jack Searle for sharing with me, and all of Dundee, their inspiring passion for the history of this city'.*

Alan Duncan needs to be thanked for his hospitality at Grey Lodge, and for help with the history of Mary Lily Walker's legacy. Thanks are also extended to the staff there.

Special mention, too, has to go to the women of **Dundee Women's Festival**, and to **Mary Henderson** and the **Dundee Women's Trail**, who have kept alive the memory of so many of Dundee's otherwise forgotten women, and amongst them, Mary Lily Walker.

Preface

Standing before the eroding red sandstone Celtic Cross that marks the grave of Mary Lily Walker, five people were brought together through the common purpose of telling a story that had remained unwritten for too long.

The date was Thursday 2nd August 2012, the sun shone brightly, and the hush of the cemetery at Balgay Hill was disturbed only by the rustle of leaves in the gusting breeze. We talked in softened tones, as many do in such a place, but every now and then an impromptu silence would break out while each of us was fixed in their own thoughts.

The final line from Professor D'Arcy Wentworth Thomson's wonderful obituary came readily to my mind:

Her name shall be honoured among the honourable women, and the rich and poor shall meet together by her grave.

And there we were, met by her grave, just as many, many rich and poor had been before, and as we considered D'Arcy's words, further lines from the same document, written in 1913, took on a greater meaning:

It is not for us to weigh and measure Lily Walker's part in this work and progress. The time is not yet come.

That time, it was decided, had now come. As the calendar approached the centenary of the death of Miss Mary Lily Walker, the time had come to weigh and measure her life and her work, just as D'Arcy Wentworth Thomson, her tutor, friend, colleague and correspondent, had prophesied in that obituary.

This is a story about a remarkable woman from a city renowned for its strong women; a woman who not only brought national attention to the desperate plight of women and children in late-Victorian Dundee, but who, through her tireless, selfless and unrelenting efforts, made a real and palpable difference to the lives of so many within the city that she held so dear. It is the story of a legacy that still survives, and indeed thrives, one hundred years after her untimely death. This is the story that has waited a long time to be told.

Chapter 1

Sunday's Child

In nineteenth-century Dundee, a Sunday morning was a good time to be born. Apart from the rattle of the occasional passing hansom cab and the gossiping of clusters of families and friends heading for their places of worship, it was a very peaceful part of the week in a town that clamoured all the other days. There were no factory noises on a Sunday; no bummers bellowing the starts and finishes of long working shifts. Nor was there the frenetic clip-clopping of passing passenger cabs, or whinnying of heavy horses drawing laden wagons of freshly landed raw jute that populated the streets every other day. As well as being the time for worship, Sunday morning was the time for weary workers, old and young, male and female, to catch up on sleep and to rest tired bodies.

Sunday morning was also the opportunity for hangovers to be worked off by the many men and women who turned to "the bottle" as a way of combating the constant strain of trying to make a living and feed a family. There were many places in Dundee where that bottle could be got. In 1860, Dundee had more pubs than bakers, had more licensed victuallers than clothing shops, and had more offences ascribed to drunkenness than all other crimes combined. Dundee had a more lenient legal system for dealing with drunkenness than Glasgow or Edinburgh. The penalty for this offence in both of the main Scottish cities was 40 shillings (£2), or fourteen days imprisonment, but offences under the 1862 Act, as they were meted in Dundee, resulted in a 5 shilling fine or twenty-four hours imprisonment at most. Apparently most of Dundee's offenders opted for the day in prison. At least, that was the penalty in most of Dundee. However, if the offence took place on the south side of Dock Street, then the Harbour Act was invoked, which led to a mandatory £5 fine, or sixty days imprisonment.[1] The clever drunk would therefore presumably stick to the north side of Dock Street. Under Dundee's relatively lenient penalty system, the same person could be charged up to five times in the same week if they took the option of imprisonment. In the nineteenth century, Dundee had many offenders of both sexes whose charge lists numbered into the hundreds.[2]

It was on Sunday 5th July 1863, at just after eleven o'clock in the morning, that Mary Lily Walker was born into Dundee. Her birth took place in the family home at 152 Perth Road just at the time when church bells were summoning their flocks. The pealing of those bells carried far in the still of a Sunday morning, and it might well have sounded like a welcoming herald to the newborn baby girl and her family. It was very calm and sunny that day, just as it had been the previous day when an afternoon parade organised by the Company of Volunteers in Dundee attracted a large impromptu audience as it marched through the centre of the town.[3]

That Saturday's procession assembled and started its march in Barrack Square. From there it had gathered quite a throng of followers, young and old, as it made its way to the Greenmarket. After a while of parading and playing in the spacious arena there, under the shadow of the Royal Arch, the procession made its way up Castle Street, past the elegant façade of the Theatre Royal, turning left at the top to jauntily snake up the High Street and onward to the Nethergate. The parade continued to the point where Nethergate became the Perth Road, and where the recently completed St Andrew's Roman Catholic Church was sited, opposite the imposing Tay Street with its many elegant houses. Here it about-turned, stopping for a few seconds to let the many enthralled and voluble children who were following form up behind. It then headed back to the High School where the performance concluded.[4] For many of the crowd the colourful parade would have been a welcome, if short-lived, diversion from the drudgery and drabness of their lowly-paid employment and their dreadful housing conditions. For others (more specifically, the better-off) it would present a vibrant, if somewhat vulgar, sight. They would choose not to follow the procession, but it would give them reason to convene with others of their own social standing in the town and they would take the opportunity to pass the time of day.

Much of the talk that Saturday would doubtlessly have concerned Queen Victoria's strapping nineteen-year-old son, Prince Alfred, and his brief visit to the town on the Monday of that week. He had arrived at Dundee station from Broughty Ferry, where his Royal Navy ship, *HMS Racoon*, was docked. He served as a lieutenant on the vessel, and, with some of the company of officers, he had taken to strolling through Dundee with the intent of visiting the Old Steeple amongst other things. The talk would have been of the huge crowd that gathered to greet him, and the gossip would have dwelt on the fact that the Prince had been forced to seek shelter in the bookshop belonging to Mr John Middleton, at 13 High Street, to escape the enthusiastic, if unruly, crowd. But they would have spoken in deeper tones about the shame of the town; the shame that Prince Alfred had rapidly marched thereafter to the station of the Dundee-Perth railway and taken the 12.45 train westbound to Stirling, just to escape these common people.[5] And most assuredly they would also have talked about the town council's hastily convened meeting on the Tuesday, at which it was decided to confer the 'freedom of the burgh' on Alfred, in the futile hope he would accept it on his return to the ship. He never did accept the honour, and his twenty-gun vessel, *Racoon*, sailed off to Wick Bay on the 9th July with little ceremony but many onlookers.[6]

That Saturday would have been heavy with gossip, and all of those who rejoiced in the parade that day, and who would have been engrossed in the atmosphere of it all, would speak to others on the Monday about the parade and about the Prince's visit. The whole town would soon know all about it, but they would have been blissfully unaware of the birth of the girl who would grow up to do so much for the benefit of the most hapless and helpless in their town.

Mary Lily was her mother's first child. Mary Anne Allen had married her husband, Thomas Walker, the previous year, and she would have been very well aware that, at the age of 39, and by the standard of the day, she had left it very late to have her first baby. Thomas was a well-to-do and highly respected solicitor in Dundee, and Mary Anne had moved from her own family home in Kirkby Lonsdale, near the rural town of Kendal in the English county of Westmoreland, to live in the bustling Scottish town where her husband made his comfortable living. At 64, Thomas was twenty-five years his wife's senior when they married in September 1862 in the Parish Church in Kirkby Lonsdale. The wedding was conducted by the Church of England vicar, Rev George Candy.[7] Their new baby daughter arrived ten months after the wedding, confirming their haste to beget.

Mary Lily, however, was not Thomas Walker's first child. In fact, Thomas had had eight children – six daughters and two sons – during his marriage to Catherine Sandeman Morison. That marriage had taken place in Dundee on the 13th July 1820 and Catherine had been a member of a very prominent family from Perth. Her tragic death from consumption in May 1835, at the young age of 35, had left Thomas a grieving widower with six children around him, as two of their children, Catherine Margaret (died aged eleven weeks) and Jane (died aged 7) had predeceased their mother.

The youngest member of his family, his daughter Grace, was 29 by the time her new baby half-sister was born. Her father, being in his mid-sixties, was a very old man (the male life expectancy in Dundee at the time was 40, and for women it was 44) and, after twenty-nine years of living without a wife, he had become very well accustomed to being a widower.[8] Nor was he without household company, for the records from the 1861 census show he lived at home with two of his daughters, Eliza and Grace, his own older sister Jean, and two female domestic servants. Certainly Thomas would not have lacked company in his comfortable domestic surroundings, but the reason he chose to marry after such a long period since his first marriage might be ascribed to the tragic events four years earlier.

On Saturday 29th May 1858 Dr William Munro left his home and surgery in Dundee's Tay Square to travel the short distance to No. 2 Airlie Place. Munro was an eminent M.D. in the city, and, as well as being a family doctor, he was also the certifying surgeon under the Factory Act in Dundee. Besides this, he acted as honorary consulting physician at the Royal Infirmary in the town. By living and practising in Dundee in the mid-eighteenth century, Dr Munro would have been very well used to the spectre of death, and on that particular day he was on his way to certify yet another fatality. He would confirm that Mr Francis Walker, the last remaining son of Thomas and his late wife Catherine, had died after ten weeks of debility and suffering, from the effects of pleurisy, at the age of 30.[9]

Francis Walker was a writer (the common term at the time for a solicitor) as was his father Thomas Walker, and his grandfather,

William Walker, before that. The Dundee Postal Directory of 1858–59 reveals that Thomas and his son Francis were in partnership, and that T & F Walker's business was situated at 116 Seagate, in the heart of the town. The coming together of Thomas and his son in their legal practice mirrored the earlier partnership of Thomas and his father William in the 1820s, a partnership based at 2 High Street, Dundee. The setting up of father-and-son businesses was common practice in the period, where it could be expected that the son would thereafter inherit the company on the retirement or death of the father. This is exactly what happened when Thomas took over the business on the event of the death of his father, William, in 1824. Their joint business had evidently flourished well enough for Thomas to go it alone. Sadly, with Francis predeceasing Thomas, the expected continuation ceased abruptly.

With the passing of Francis, Thomas Walker was faced with a predicament all too common in this period in history. His other son from his first marriage, William, had died six years earlier in 1852. He too had been involved in the family business, where he had been employed as a solicitor's clerk. With the death of both sons, Thomas knew that the lucrative and successful business might effectively close on his own death, as it could only be handed on to a male heir. As well as his desire to maintain the thriving business, the monies accrued from his practice were keeping his three remaining daughters in comfort, with no need to resort to paid employment. Although Thomas had formed a temporary business partnership with James Ewing after the death of Francis, this was probably little more than a coming together of their names, rather than their business interests, and he made a decision that he should marry again in the attempt to have another son who might take on his mantle.

Whilst the idea of marrying for the sake of procreation may seem callous to modern sensibilities, in the mid-nineteenth century this would have been considered a logical, legitimate and almost laudable decision. To say there was no deep affection between Thomas and his new wife Mary Anne might be incorrect, and difficult to substantiate, but the fact that a legally witnessed pre-nuptial agreement was sought and drawn up by both parties in the union would suggest that a high level of pragmatism accompanied any fondness. However, pre-nuptial agreements were reasonably commonplace in Victorian times, when they were often termed "pre-marriage settlements", and they were most specifically used in cases, just as this, where children from a previous marriage were to be financially protected.[10]

In the days leading up to the birth of Mary Lily, Thomas must have been every bit as anxious as his new wife. For her there was the worrying prospect of bearing a first child, exacerbated by her being at such an advanced physical age, an age by which many women in Dundee were ailing or becoming infirm. Presumably though, this would have been assuaged by the prospect of motherhood, and the sense of maternal fulfilment which would probably have been amongst her main reasons for marrying and moving to this very different environment. But the apprehension of her husband, Thomas, was two-fold. He would have been very concerned for the welfare of both his wife and her baby, but he may well have also worried about the low probability of this child being the son he craved. History pointed the odds at a daughter; six of his eight earlier offspring were female, and Dundee's population had a very high proportion of females to males. Dundee was a woman's town for more reasons than one.

Thomas would have organised a doctor to attend his wife in the lead-up to the delivery of their baby. It would not have been Dr Monro, who had attended the dying Francis, for he, too, had subsequently died. It may have been James Christie M.D. who had since taken on the Tay Square practice and residence. Wealthier families like the Walkers would employ and pay for the services of a doctor, rather than opt for any of the midwives who were numerous in the town. There were five listed in the *Dundee Directory* for 1863, though in actuality there were probably many times those numbers. They offered a very worthwhile service to the needy and lower classes, but they were not trained, governed, licensed, or even monitored in any way, and many did their "duties" for free.

At the arrival of baby Walker, the doctor would presumably have had the task of telling Thomas Walker that his wife had successfully delivered a healthy baby girl. How Thomas reacted to this news can only be imagined. But as a practised father, it seems reasonable to believe that he received the news with stoicism and good grace. How he felt inside is another matter. Did he rue not being granted a son? The fact that he took twenty days before registering the birth of his daughter in the Registrar's Office in Barrack Street may or may not be pertinent. Certainly he had never had to register a birth previously (that mandatory procedure had not been enforced in Scotland until 1855) but he had managed to register the death of poor Francis within three days of that event. It was a sign of the times that death registration had a maximum of seven days while birth could be registered up to six weeks after the event.[11] This six week period would be reduced to twenty-one days in 1907, and Mary Lily's work would be influential in this national reduction in the number of days permitted for the recording of any birth. The period difference between death and birth registrations remains to this day. In one of life's cruel ironies, *The Dundee Courier and Argus* of 10th July 1863 reported on the case of a child having been abandoned at the door of a house in Airlie Place, not 200 yards from the Walker household. The baby was reckoned to be less than a week old, and could well have been born on the same day as Mary Lily. The child was an unwanted boy. What subsequently happened to this abandoned baby was not reported.

Thomas and Mary Anne would eventually have a son. Arthur John Thomas Walker was born on the 22nd April 1867, at the family home that was by then Sunnybank, 61 Magdalen Yard Road, Dundee. Thomas was 69 years of age, and his wife 43, by the time their last child arrived. Whilst the move to the imposing and much bigger house showed that the family finances were doing very well, the birth of their son may well have had a permanent and damaging effect on Mary Anne's physical health. There were four years between Mary Lily's birth and the birth of her brother. Given their eagerness to have a son and heir, this four year gap may suggest that Mary Anne had health problems during that period, or possibly suffered pregnancies which failed to reach the end of gestation.

Thomas must have realised that his newborn son's appearance had come too late to give the benefit he had yearned for. Thomas would be in his late eighties before Arthur might leave school for university, and over 90 before he could possibly enter the family's legal business. With this thought in mind, Thomas entered into a new business partnership with a young Dundee solicitor named John Duff Bruce who was asked to pay £350 for the privilege.[12] This was a more complete partnership than any Thomas had previously courted, and, after Thomas's death, Bruce would take over the business. Bruce would also marry Thomas's daughter Eliza, despite her being six years older.

൸   ൙

Mary Lily was born into a world strongly bound to social and gender divisions; the lifestyle and life expectancies for a man were very different to those for a woman. Britain was also in a state of prolonged mourning for Queen Victoria's husband, Prince Albert, who had died in the December of 1861. Across the entire country, changes brought about by technological advances in both agriculture and industry were having a great impact on society. Better machinery and improved practises meant that fewer people were needed to work the land. This resulted in people being pushed away, or even ejected, from the rural lives that their forefathers had always lived. It saw them being sucked into urban areas where work of sorts existed and labour demand seemed insatiable. Inevitably, suitable accommodation within these urban areas did not always keep up with this mass movement of working people and their families. Nowhere was more affected by this irreversible trend than the town of Dundee.

Dundee's 30,000-strong population rose incredibly in the fifty years from 1821. By 1831 it had risen by half to over 45,000. Effectively, a third of Dundee's population in 1831 were strangers to each other, and strangers to the town. By 1841 another 21,000 souls needed to find work, food, and housing, when the population was recorded at over 66,000. By the time baby Mary Lily Walker was added to the count, Dundee had almost 100,000 of a population. Eight years later, in the 1871 census, there were no fewer than 122,000 people living in Dundee.[13] Added to that, it was estimated that, at any given time, over 3000 seamen would be in Dundee, presumably sleeping on the many ships that kept the harbours and docks busy.[14] In fifty years the population of Dundee had therefore risen four-fold. Demand for housing completely outstripped supply, and in Dundee, a town that had eschewed any real improvements, the result was chronic overcrowding, dreadful sanitation problems and dire living conditions, which inevitably brought about hardship, sickness and death.

On the face of it, the level of employment that was created in Dundee should have led to the creation of a great deal of wealth. It had, but that wealth never was distributed equitably. It was said Dundee had more millionaires per head of population than any other town in Britain, but there was also the other extreme: widespread poverty as bad as, if not worse than, any other industrial city in Britain. This was the Dundee that awaited Mary Lily Walker. Her own family, by good fortune, were on the "right side" of the wealth divide. Yet the depths that humanity could sink to were never far from the sight, or even the nose, of Mary Lily.

One thing, above all others, allowed the factory and mill owners to exploit their workforces – the great fluctuations in demand for the manufactured linen and jute products on which Dundee pinned its hopes. On the day Mary Lily was born, half-a-world away in America, the Civil War which was tearing that nation asunder had moved to the area around Gettysburg. The dreadful losses of life of July 1863 has become forever symbolic and iconic following U.S. President Abraham Lincoln's famous, and oft-times quoted, Gettysburg Address. This battle may have been viewed with sadness around the world, but nothing boosted the textile trade more than war or the prospect of conflict somewhere around the globe. Linen and jute for sails or for tents, for the covering of wagons or holding sand in bags, were both in huge demand in the late-eighteenth century and there were many other fields of conflict besides America, like the Crimean and Boer Wars. Dundee always benefitted from conflict and war. If the order books of the textile mills were full then all those in Dundee who could, including pre-teenage children, would turn out to work.[15] In the 1860s, when Mary Lily arrived, Dundee was going through a particularly busy spell in the demand for textiles, and the problems of unemployment were not anticipated.

When the mills were less busy in Dundee there was no compunction about cutting wages and paying off workers. When there was a diminution in the workforce, it was almost always the men who would be paid off first. This was simply because women were paid less, and women tended to accept what little there was on offer far more readily than male employees. Dundee became, and remained for three-quarters of a century, a town where women and children worked when their men-folk could get no employment. This situation was exacerbated by the fact that there were far more women than men in Dundee, particularly from the ages of 20 to 40, and also that the influx of Irish immigrants to Dundee consisted mostly of women. This contrasted with the state of affairs in Glasgow, which also saw a huge boost to its population coming from Ireland, except the Irish incomers to Glasgow were predominantly men.[16]

Like Glasgow, Dundee also found itself housing many people who had moved by necessity from rural environments, trying to find work to earn money and provide a roof over their heads. Many of those who moved into Dundee were from the hamlets and glens of Angus to the north, or from Fife to the south, but many flocked from the Highlands of Scotland, and, like the Irish, they seemed happy to stick together whenever possible. Wherever they emanated from, they all seemed to be resolved to make the most of the cramped and overcrowded housing, and to view any sort of work as infinitely preferable to no work at all.[17] The bulk of the people coming into the town, no matter how destitute they felt and how harsh their previous situations had been, must have left homes in the country where living space and fresh air were the norm. Now they had moved into a very different and frightening "new" world. Dundee's medieval housing consisted of areas of pends, closes, and back-lands: all very dark, dank and forbidding. What might have seemed like an orderly façade of tenement flats from the street often hid a back-world of crowded higgledy-piggledy blocks of flatted houses. At the best of times these back-lands were tight and cramped, and their proximity to each other offered a paucity of sunlight or fresh air; in the inevitable overcrowding that came from the huge increase in population these must have seemed utterly hellish. Ubiquitous squalor, a total lack of privacy, very unhealthy air, and all types of anti-social behaviour would be evident. But worst of all, with the utter lack of sewerage, dreadfully inadequate toilet provision and unavailability of running water, Dundee, in 1863, and for a long time afterwards, was in a state of sanitary chaos.[18]

The Public Health Act of 1867 saw police officers appointed to the new posts of Sanitary Inspectors. This was a Scotland-wide initiative, but nowhere was in greater need of improvement than the town of Dundee. This town had virtually no drainage, and what meagre provision there was amounted to stone-built rubble channels that allowed noxious liquids to escape into the ground to poison the earth, and accompanying fumes to escape into the air. The only sewers were confined to main thoroughfares. There were only five "water closets" in the whole of Dundee by 1867, three of which were in hotels and the others in private houses, and all five of these depended on water fetched in pails in order to be flushed. Some houses, and some workplaces, had brick-built "privies", perhaps a thousand for the whole town, which allowed human waste to fall into specially dug holes of up to five feet in depth. Dundee also had fourteen public lavatories, each of which had between ten and thirty open wooden-seated holes with all waste material again falling into trenches which were dug around five feet deep. All of these needed to be emptied daily, so men were employed as scavengers to undertake this unwholesome task. Wearing sea-boots, these employees had the unenviable job of removing all manner of waste from these pits and removing this material to the main street where it was dumped and left until horse-drawn transport would take it away. The same applied to middens in the backyards of tenement buildings where waste was thrown into ash or straw heaps, before the scavengers performed their nightly collections. Waste was also left in pails by residents to be emptied directly into carts. These pails could be emptied only once in twenty-four hours, and would remain in houses, with the resultant odours and flies, until collection time.[19] The sights and smells in the streets prior to the carts taking away the effluvium can, thankfully, hardly be imagined. Added to this was *'the indecencies of children and others which were constantly to be met with in the streets, lanes, courts, and entries'* because of the inadequacy, or unavailability, of public toilets.[20] Mary Anne Allen, coming from the small agricultural town of Kirkby Lonsdale, must have been appalled by this aspect of urban life in her new situation.

There was no piped water into household properties at this time; all water would have had to be carried in pails, and carrying these to the tops of tenement blocks must have been a struggle. Queues at standpipes and water troughs must have been constant by day, and it is possible the water would have been recycled, with washing, cooking and flushing being done with the same pail-full. How fastidious people would have been about washing themselves and their properties when it was such a chore to fetch water can only be imagined. But between the lack of drains, the nauseous fumes, the disgusting practice in the removal of human effluent and the dearth of running water it is easy to see how infectious disease and death were constant visitors to the households of the town.[21]

Mary Lily Walker would never have had to carry water pails, let alone waste pails. The domestic servants of her father's household would have carried out those tasks, along with disinfecting the property and scrupulous scrubbing of the doorstep. Most of the water to the Walker household, though, was probably purchased by the barrel-load, from one of the many carters who brought supplies into the town to the wealthier citizens. But young Mary Lily would have witnessed the pail-carrying practice at houses near her own, as this was a chore often done by children and teenagers.

The infant Mary Lily had a nursemaid, Jane Johnston, who came from Glamis, who would be charged with walking the child in the areas of freshest air.[22] But Mary Lily would never be far from the sights, sounds and smells of the less salubrious parts of the town. The Dundee street called Step Row, which leads from Magdalen Yard Road to Perth Road, was immediately next to the family house at Sunnybank. In the 1871 census it is recorded that a certain '*poet and tragedian*', William McGonagall, with his wife Jean and seven children, lived in a two-roomed house at No. 41. Although it was round the corner, it was effectively next door but one to the Walker abode. In that same census it is recorded that, in the shared close where McGonagall dwelt, there was a two-roomed house with twenty-seven named inhabitants.[23]

The Improvement Act of 1871 would begin to change the face of Dundee, though it took the best part of forty years before most houses were piped and linked to running water, and before all permanent toilets were connected to the new sewerage and drainage systems. It was in that period that Mary Lily would be moved to become more and more involved in improving the lot of the most desperately under-privileged of her fellow citizens.

ဢ ဢ

The lighting of houses in the Dundee of 1863 was achieved largely with oil lamps, but The Dundee Gas Company, and its rival, the imaginatively named The New Dundee Gas Company, were providing more and more houses with gas. However, a new option, though one that would take a long time to fulfil its potential, would be witnessed by the Dundee people in 1867. The electric light was demonstrated to the populace of Dundee during the British Association for the Advancement of Science visit to the city in that year. In the week of September during which the Society held its 37th annual conference, displays of this new and wondrous lighting phenomenon were put on at Dundee High School and in Dundee's High Street. The awe-struck people of Dundee flocked to these demonstrations, and there was undoubtedly a very healthy appreciation of the worth of science in the town. Thomas Walker would almost certainly have gone with Mary Lily and the rest of his family to see this spectacle. His interest in science is evident in his visit to the Social Science Congress in Edinburgh in the October of 1863.[24] He was also a subscribing director of Dundee High School where many of the specialist lectures were to take place.

This conference was very successful in the number of attendees, the number of new members generated (including many individuals from the wealthy textile manufacturing families) and the number of highly eminent people who came to Dundee to speak to rapt audiences. The British Association for the Advancement of Science had visited Scotland on five previous occasions, but this was the first visit to a town without a university. The Duke of Buccleuch was appointed as Chairman of this meeting, and the only sadness was the news that the famous scientist, Michael Faraday, who had visited Dundee in the past to preach to the Glasite Church in King Street, had died just a few weeks before the British Association's Dundee visit.[25]

Whilst this event fascinated the people of Dundee, and would certainly have interested Thomas Walker, it was to have an even bigger effect on the life of his youngest daughter. The event would turn out to be the main catalyst for the opening of University College in Dundee in 1883, where the young Mary Lily would enrol as a student in the new institution's first intake and become one of the first women in all of Scotland to undertake university courses opened to both sexes.[26]

The Albert Institute in Dundee was specifically opened to accommodate the 1867 conference. Only part of the present building was available at that time, and the Society's lectures had to be held in other places, such as the high school, some church halls, and in the Kinnaird Hall. In keeping with the social mores of the time, the Society permitted no women members, although there were women addressing the conference. One speaker in particular, Mrs (Eliza) Lynn Linton, was the first female journalist in Britain and had been a newspaper correspondent in Paris for some time. As well as being a novelist of worth, and a friend to many of the literary greats of the time (especially Elizabeth and Robert Browning, and Charles Dickens, to whom she sold her house), Mrs Linton was known for her knowledge of the French scene. The Paris Exhibition earlier in 1867 had brought alarming news to British ears of the technological advances in electricity and physics which seemed to put continental Europe at the forefront of scientific advancement. Mrs Linton spoke about the French developments and the other continental advancements in scientific discovery. This added fuel to the growing concern amongst the great and the good of the science world about educational practices in Britain.

Many other luminaries of British society chose to visit Dundee for the meeting. Included in this list were the writer Charles Kingsley and the poet Robert Browning. The conference strongly recommended that both university and school education in Britain should be widened and improved. In particular it needed to be much more scientifically-orientated if Britain was to retain its vaunted position as leader in industrial advancements. The Dundee textile manufacturers amongst the membership listened, concurred, and, with other eminent citizens, began to draw up new plans for further-education facilities in Dundee.[27]

The buzz throughout Dundee in 1867 was great, and would certainly not have been lost on the four-year-old Mary Lily. Every hotel would have been filled and many of the important people would have been staying as guests in the homes of Dundee's wealthy elite. Who knows, maybe Thomas Walker, already a director of Dundee High School, would have taken one or more of these visitors as guests into his home, given his own interest in science. Special cabs were laid on at the railway station to transfer visitors to an established meeting point in Panmure Street, where special messengers, resplendent in broad white armbands for identification, were made available by the town to safely escort these guests to their accommodation or lectures. These white arm-banded escorts would have been a novelty as they traversed the town with the honoured visitors.[28] The local newspapers were full of positive comments about the great success of Dundee's event, and it was to warm appreciation and approbation that the society laid on a special lecture one evening to let the *operatives* of the city (this meant the "common workers") sample the wonderfully informative talks. This special lecture was held in the Kinnaird Hall to a completely packed house and the Duke of Buccleuch was given a huge and resounding cheer from those who were fortunate enough to gain admission.[29]

1867 was also the year when an International Chess Tournament was held in Dundee. This took place between the 4th and the 13th September and was held in the boardroom of the Caledonian Railway Company. The recognised world-champion, Wilhelm Steinitz, headed an excellent and international field of competitors and the Dundee Chess Club received plaudits from the competitors for their running of affairs.[30] Dundee, consequently, was at the forefront of much press coverage in Britain and further afield. But whilst this town of huge contrasts was enjoying the experience of holding such prestigious events simultaneously and very successfully, there was an outbreak of cholera sweeping through the overcrowded parts of the city, wreaking death and grief on an already beleaguered section of the population. 1860 to 1870 was a particularly bad decade for epidemics of typhus, gastric fever and smallpox.[31]

In 1865 alone there were over a thousand cases of typhus recorded.[32] There was also the occasional case of cholera, a disease that was more prevalent because of the unusually warm weather. The death rate increased, especially amongst infants and young children, and it was due to the high numbers of incomers rather than the rate of indigenous childbirth that Dundee's population continued to escalate. The wealthy and elite amongst Dundee's population were less affected by diseases and death. They were not living in the same areas of the town as the hoi polloi. They were building greater and bigger houses to the east of the city towards West Ferry or Broughty Ferry, or flitting far west to the cleaner air of the Perth Road. Some had made the move across the water to peaceful Fife and endured the two-mile commute across the Tay Estuary rather than live in the foul-smelling energy of the town. Consequently, they and their families were relatively unaffected by the epidemics of disease.[33] But whilst the mixing-pot of incoming families to Dundee lived with the daily threat of illness, and the daily sight of death around them, any united opposition to working conditions or combined defence against squalor and resultant disease were almost non-existent.

The Victorian paradigm of the wealthy and well-to-do doling out charity to the poorest and least able in society was very evident in Dundee. By the time Mary Lily was born, many of the wives and daughters of the wealthier families were involved in charitable works. Victorian Britain was brimming with philanthropic posturing.[34] Whether this was done solely in order to bring benefit to the desperate, or whether this acted as some sort of salve for the conscience of those who benefited financially from the deplorable living conditions of the under-classes, is a moot point. Charity may even have served as a way of keeping up with other elite families in an almost competitive manner. But whatever the reason, these do-gooders certainly brought some attention to very many underprivileged and "fallen" characters. Whether many of those Dundee individuals who were on the receiving end of all the "moral guidance" actually appreciated it is unknown. From 1850 more and more charitable and benevolent institutions, with committees of well-meaning women, were being listed in the Dundee Postal Directories.[35] Mary Lily's half-sister, Eliza, was active on a few of these, and at the time of her new sister's birth she was serving on the Ladies Committee of the Dundee Industrial Schools Society which had been formed in 1846.[36]

The commitment to charitable works and service to improve society was very evident in the family of Thomas Walker. Eliza remained on the committee of the Dundee Industrial Schools Society for over thirty years, and she also served for a while on the committees of the Royal Orphanage, when it was situated in nearby Small's Wynd. She also served on the committee of the Dundee Ladies' Union. Grace Walker, her younger sister, also joined the committee of the Dundee Industrial Schools Society, as well as the Dundee & District Female Rescue Home in Union Place. Mary Lily's mother was listed in records under her married name of Mrs Thos Walker, and she served on the Ladies' committee of '*The Home*'. This was a charitable institution, originally set up in 1848 in Dundee's Paton's Lane under the patronage of the Duchess of Kent, for the '*Reformation of Females*'. The problems of drunkenness and prostitution amongst women may have been mirrored in other industrial towns, but in Dundee it was seen to be a social blight and particularly rife. The premises of this institution moved three times in thirty years, but always to different addresses in Paton's Lane. Thomas Walker himself had been in office as Factor to '*The Home*' until his resignation in 1874 due to ailing health. This was a paid sinecure in contrast to his wife's charitable work.[37] His son-in-law to be, John Duff Bruce, as partner in the legal business, took on the position in his stead. Mary Lily was therefore brought up in a household where service to those who were considered in need of help in Dundee was earnestly supported.

In supporting these institutions, members of the Walker family would be networking with Dundee's wealthiest families. '*The Home*' had several titled Ladies providing support. Female members of the Baxters, the Gourlays, the Coxes and the Grimmonds, amongst a group of renowned family names, were liberally interspersed throughout disparate charitable committees in Dundee, as well as in the Paton's Lane establishment. Male members of Dundee's wealthiest community were also to be found listed on the boards of these "good works".[38]

Specific acts of benevolence proved very popular. For example, in September 1863, two months after the birth of Mary Lily, Baxter Park in the town's Arbroath Road was opened, and a tremendous crowd turned up for the event. The park was officially opened by the Prime Minister of the time, Earl Russell, and it is estimated that 70,000 people turned up to watch.[39] In terms of the proportion of the population of Dundee, this was a massive turnout, and the gratitude and approbation of the citizens was evinced in the huge number of individuals who contributed to the fund to provide a statue of the benefactor, Sir David Baxter. Baxter Brothers, his company, was by this time the biggest producer of linen products in the entire world, and the town of Dundee was now Britain's largest importer of flax.

შ ლ

Mary Lily Walker was born into a town of great contrasts and contradictions. The railway system, the invention that was transforming life and industry across the length and breadth of Britain, was growing at an astonishing rate. So popular was this new method of transportation that tracks were being laid to all sorts of places. Much land was given over to this progression, and the railway developments had necessarily encroached into Dundee's foreshore. Areas of reclamation altered the river shoreline, and in the area immediately in front of the Walker family house, access to the beach and to the shore was obstructed by rail lines coming from Perth.[40] By way of recompense a new public park had been developed at Magdalen Green. Also planned, but not to start for another few years, was the most ambitious railway project of the age in the entire world: The Tay Railway Bridge.

Dundee of the time had some fine new buildings, including the Royal Exchange Building which had been finished, after three years of construction, in 1856. St Andrew's Roman Catholic Church, in Nethergate, built in 1836, was competing with St Paul's Episcopalian Church at the top of Seagate (built between 1852–55) to be the most impressive religious edifice.[41] Many new church buildings had, in fact, been built in Dundee around this period, and their proliferation was partly due to the fact that Dundee, like so many other towns in Scotland, offered a number of different options and separate denominations where the populace could worship and express their faith. The *Dundee Directory* for 1864 lists a total of forty places of worship. Eight churches belonged to the Established Church of Scotland. There were thirteen Free Churches, including one that was Gaelic speaking. Seven United Presbyterian, six Congregationalist, four Episcopal and two Roman Catholic churches were dotted around the city. You could also find Reformed Presbyterians, United Original Seceders, Baptists, Glasites, Old Scotch Independents, Evangelical Unionists,

Wesleyan Methodists, Primitive Methodists, the Christian Church, the United Christian Church, the Disciples of Christ and even Mormonites, also known as Latter Day Saints.[42]

This diverse collection of religious institutions reflects the numbers of incomers to Dundee. The growth of Roman Catholicism was helped by the Irish immigrants whilst the number of Free Churches, and particularly the Gaelic-speaking one, are testament to the influx of people from the Highlands and North West of Scotland. A particularly interesting church, one that played a part in the Walker dynasty, was the Glasite Church, which sat in Dundee's King Street next to St Andrews Church.

Like other industrial towns, as well as erecting new places of worship and public buildings, Dundee needed to consider how to dispose of its dead. The population growth meant that the existing burial grounds were inadequate to cope with the ever-increasing numbers of people dying in the city. There was also the problem of the shifting boundaries of Dundee. The rapidly growing town meant that the old burial grounds, which had at one time been on the outskirts, were now situated in the centre of town amongst the living. These old burial grounds were situated at Logie, and at Constitution Road, at St Andrews Church, St Peters, and at Roodyards, but the biggest and best known was The Howff in Dundee's Ward Road.[43]

The Howff was located on ground donated to the town by Mary Queen of Scots in the 1560s. The area had once been an orchard belonging to the Franciscan Monastery and the name was an old Scots word for "a meeting place". At the time of the Queen's bequest it sat outside the town, but by the nineteenth century it was very much in the centre. New cemeteries were needed, both to accommodate the city's increasing number of funerals and to take the disposal of the dead away from the population centre. The Western Cemetery, commercially owned at the time and situated well out of the centre on the Perth Road, opened in 1845. It was followed by the Eastern Necropolis, situated on Arbroath Road on twenty acres of ground purchased in 1862 by Dundee Corporation for £9000. The town also purchased land for the Western Necropolis, more commonly termed "Balgay Hill", and the twenty-five acres bought for £7594 saw its first burial in 1869. Both of these town-owned new cemeteries were increased in size by further land acquisitions and by the end of the century the "Eastern" sat on forty acres whilst Balgay Hill was a hundred acre site. Within fifty years of their opening, these two cemeteries had accepted over 135,000 bodies for interment.

The Howff closed for funerals in 1858[44], save for a few existing lair-holders, and Francis Walker was the last of Walker family to be interred there. This decision to close the Howff must have given Thomas a great deal of concern and grief. This ancient burial ground held the bodies of his first wife, Catherine, and five of their children: Jane (b.1823 d.1830), Catherine Margaret (b.1833 d.1833), a second daughter named Jane (b.1831 d.1845), William (b.1825 d.1852) and Francis (b.1828 d.1858). Also in the same area of the Howff, next to the Walker gravestones, was the burial place of John Glas (1695–1773), the minister from Tealing who left the Church of Scotland to form the Glasite Church. The proximity of Glas's grave to that of the Walker family was no coincidence, symbolising, as it did, the historical and religious links that had existed between them.[45]

With the closing of the Howff, Thomas was forced to make different burial arrangements for himself and the rest of his family and in 1860 he purchased a lair comprising of six coffin spaces at the Western Cemetery on the Perth Road. Within two years this new plot would be used for the interment of his sister, Jean, who had died a few months before Thomas married his second wife. Two years later, just a year after the birth of Mary Lily, Thomas's last remaining sister, Elizabeth, died and was buried in the second space in the "Western". Thus, by August 1864, when he was aged 66, Thomas had buried the last of his nine siblings, five of his nine children and his first wife. He was to join his sisters in this family lair in due course, but his second wife, Mary Anne Allen, would not be laid beside him, and neither would their children, Mary Lily and Arthur.

This was the Dundee that awaited the newly born Mary Lily Walker in 1863. Before her schooling was completed, she would witness a city where astounding achievements and great building developments walked hand-in-hand with utmost destitution, a deplorable death rate, and all manner of grief and hardships.

Chapter 2

Genesis

The Walkers and the Allens knew each other long before Mary Lily's mother and father were married. Their home towns of Dundee and Kirkby Lonsdale were unlike each other in every way, except that they had a connection through religion. Dundee, with its enviable position on the north bank of the impressive River Tay, had always looked to the river and the sea to provide sustenance and employment: initially through fishing, then through trading, ship building and whaling. The deep channel of the river was also key to the landing of foreign products, such as flax and raw jute, which Dundee's labour force spun and wove into products which went to both home and overseas markets in great quantity. Even the manufacture of marmalade, synonymous with the Keillour factory in Dundee where it was said to have been "invented", came from a cargo of inedible sour oranges that were landed at the harbour.

Kirkby Lonsdale was a long way from the sea, and no textile factory ever polluted its skyline. It was as old as Dundee, with a proud and ancient tradition of being a market town. Livestock markets were the main source of commerce, although a water-powered textile-printing mill, and some small woollen mills added to the available employment. At the time that Mary Anne Allen left her family home to move with her new husband to his Scottish home, Kirkby Lonsdale had an estimated population of 1300[46]; this was little more than one-hundredth the size of Dundee's.

Sited inland, betwixt the Yorkshire Dales and the Lake District, Kirkby Lonsdale grew up around its ancient parish church, and the very name of the town suggests that religion always played a big part. Indeed, in the seventeenth century it was said to be a place where *'people round about repair to church and mercate'*.[47] Wesley's Methodists had built a meetinghouse in the town by 1778. This was replaced by a new chapel, built in 1834, which remains in use as the oldest Methodist church in the Kendal area. An Independent (Congregational) chapel had been established around 1815, though it was to close in the 1930s.[48] One other religious group who met and worshipped were the Inghamites, named after the founder, Bernard Ingham, and this group played a large part in the religious life of the Allen family.

In 1759, Benjamin Ingham read John Glas's *The testimony of the King of Martyrs concerning His kingdom*, and Robert Sandeman's *Letters on Theron and Aspasio*. Glas and Sandeman were well-known in religious circles for their different, more scriptural approach to Presbyterianism. His own church was struggling for supporters, so Ingham contacted Glas and his son-in-law, Sandeman, in the hope of forming some sort of religious union, something he hoped would prop up his flagging Inghamite Church. In 1760 he sent two of his ministers, James Allen and William Batty, on a secretive mission to Scotland to learn first-hand about Glasite practices. They reported back to Ingham in October 1761, but though Ingham warmed to the idea of some sort of connection, he had no intention of relinquishing his position as *'General Overseer'*. One of his two envoys, Batty, opted to support Ingham, but Allen returned to Scotland. He converted to the Sandemanians, named after Glas's son-in-law, and became an Elder. He went back to England, moving to Yorkshire as a missionary, and there he converted several Inghamite congregations to Sandemanianism. Allen thereafter moved to Kirkby Lonsdale. Inghamites had been meeting in the town from late-eighteenth century, but with Allen's efforts they reverted to Sandemanianism, and a Sandemanian chapel was built in the market town in 1828. This had closed by 1873 and ultimately became a public library. The James Allen who had brought his new-found religion to Yorkshire and Westmoreland was the grandfather of Mary Anne Allen, who would one day be the mother of Mary Lily Walker.[49]

John Glas was a minister from Tealing, a village just to the north of Dundee, who had been educated in both Perth and St Andrews. He was ousted from the Church of Scotland in 1730 due to his doctrinal views. He was opposed to state intervention in the Church ('*My Kingdom is not of this world*' (John 18:36) was his justification) and so set up his own church in Dundee. Three years later he set up a chapel in Perth after he had secured a congregation. He fathered fifteen children, and, in 1737, the oldest of his daughters, Katharine, married Robert Sandeman. It was Sandeman who went on to establish churches with broadly the same ideology of Sandemanianism in England and America. Glas confined himself to Perth for a time, before returning to Dundee where he died in 1773 at the age of 78. He would certainly have witnessed the building of the octagonal Glasite Church in Dundee's King Street, but there is contention over whether it was finished before his death. At the forefront, amongst the many prominent families in Dundee who supported the Glasite Church, was the Walker family. Mary Lily's great grandfather on her father's side was John Walker, a hosier in the Murraygate, and he would be the one who led the Walker family into the Glasite Church. John also held the prestigious role of Boxmaster, or treasurer, to the Glovers Guild. It was a role that, on his death, he would pass to his son, William, and after his death it became the privileged holding of Lily's father, Thomas.[50]

In the late eighteenth and early nineteenth centuries the Presbyterian Church was showing signs of splitting, something which did come about in 1843. Most of the people of Scotland, almost all of whom would have attended church, were very aware of this situation. Many Scottish people attended more than one church and much of the information of the day, as well as much of the gossip, was passed in this way. Dundee would have been no different from anywhere else in the country in this respect. As well as being a Glasite, attending its strangely shaped chapel, John Walker, through his office in the Glover's Guild, would have been required to attend St Andrews Church. The distance between the Glasite Chapel and St Andrews Church was no more than a few yards, both being sited in the same grounds. St Andrews Church of Scotland had opened around 1774, and John Walker would have been one of the Office Bearers tasked with choosing the first minister for this 136ft high edifice. The town council in Dundee at the time refused to have anything to do with the cost of this new church, so the Kirk Session and the Nine Trades of Dundee shared the cost. This part-ownership situation meant that Office Bearers on the Trades, including the Glovers, were expected to attend their church.[51] This doubling of church attendance is something that would go on to affect Mary Lily's grandfather, William, and also her father, Thomas.

Mary Anne Allen was the daughter of John Allen (1790–1872) and Jane Carr (1790–1837). At the time of her marriage to Thomas Walker in 1862, Mary Anne lived at Stricklandgate in Kirkby Lonsdale, with her brothers James and Oswald, and her sisters Elizabeth and Jane. They had a boarder staying in the house, who was an apprentice draper in the shop in Kendal owned by James, and they kept two servant girls to look after their needs. They were a wealthy family, their father having worked as the Bank Manager in Wilson's Bank, which was owned by an uncle. Oswald was never a very healthy man, having what was described as *'a constitutional malady'*. He was a well-known hymn writer, as indeed was his father. Oswald wrote a book, containing no less than 148 hymns, which was published in London in 1862, the same year as his sister's marriage to the solicitor from Dundee. Oswald worked in his father's bank from 1848, when his health allowed it, and was committed to helping *'with works of benevolence and mercy among the poor, the sick, and the suffering'*. Oswald died in 1878, and Mary Lily would have been at the funeral in Kirkby Lonsdale along with her mother. Oswald, who had lived to be 62, had a Scottish connection of sorts, in that he resided in Glasgow for three years from 1843. Such was his ability as a hymn writer that he was included in Edwin Hatfield's book, *Poets of the Church*, which was published in 1884. Some are still popular today.

Oswald's brother, James Allen (1814–1896), with whom Mary Lily often stayed during summers and Christmases, was also a regular and prominent church-goer and an extremely generous man. He started his working career as an apprentice draper, along with a cousin named John Wilson (possibly the son of the bank owner). He spent some time in London before returning to establish himself in the drapery business in Kendal. Such was his love of his work that he never retired and worked until his death in 1896 at the age of 82. He gifted £25,000 pounds to the town, an enormous sum for the time, and the Allen Technical Institute was opened in 1912 as a result. Thomas Walker had a great deal of respect for James, who was appointed *'curator'* for Mary Lily and her brother Arthur in Thomas's will.[52]

The Allen family remained staunch supporters of Sandemanianism, so prevalent in their part of the world.

The Walker family remained loyal to the Glasite faith. It was almost certainly through this religious connection that Thomas and Mary Anne met in the first place. The burgeoning of the railway network in Britain would have helped to make their tryst much more possible, and the Allen connection to Dundee through Mary Anne's grandfather James (1734–1804) would have meant that the families had known each other for three generations. Thus, a God-fearing and church-going family brought Mary Lily Walker up to be generous in thought and deed, whilst being able to enjoy the comforts of wealth. However, being wealthy could sometimes cause rifts in a religious community.

The Glasites did not believe in the accumulation of wealth, and neither did the Sandemanians. Glasites met twice every Sunday. They were known for the feeding of soup to their congregation – the term *'The Kail-Kirk'* was used often – and for the washing of each other's feet. The Church was strict in its expectations of parishioners, and was quick to banish those who failed to live by its standards. These strict rules were paralleled in the Sandemanian Church, and, as both the Walkers in Dundee and the Allens in Kirkby Lonsdale flourished as wealthy middle-class families, the tensions between them and their relative Churches must have grown. The 1843 Disruption of The Church of Scotland brought another element to the religious scene which would have ramifications for Glasites and the Walker family. The state church, the Church of Scotland, was felt to be letting itself be politically influenced in many ways, and the subject of patronage brought matters to a head. Presbyterian principles were based on the congregation, through its chosen elders, having the power to decide who would be appointed Minister in each Parish. By the early 1800s many churches were having Ministers appointed by wealthy parishioners through a form of patronage, or influence was being wielded outwith the parish on who would be appointed to Ministry. The Free Church of Scotland was formed from the schism, and those who wanted a return to original values and a more scripturally led ethos joined the breakaway group. In many ways The Free Church stood for similar doctrinal issues as the Glasites, but without quite the same immutable rules. At this point the future of John Glas's Church looked bleak when many families, including Thomas Walker's, opted to attend the Free Church. When St Peter's opened shortly afterwards, in Dundee's Perth Road, this was The Free Church of Scotland that Thomas and his family chose for worship.

At around the same time, the Sandemanian Church began to see a distinct dwindling in numbers of adherents. Times were changing in English religious adherence too, for several reasons. The demographic change in Scotland, where industry was drawing people into work opportunities, was mirrored in England. This changed church-going habits and the growing towns were struggling to cope with the housing of the many variations to the Protestant theme. Queen Victoria's reign, too, witnessed a public re-assessment of the Church, and a creep towards secular thoughts. The Sandemanian Church was now viewed as "old-fashioned" and its strict and archaic rules were beginning to put off adherents. By the late 1830s many of the English followers of Sandeman were looking to other churches to give prayer and to worship. This tide reached more rural parts more slowly, but within a few years the Allen family, like so many of the wealthier families, reverted to the established Church which Victoria now headed: the Church of England.

Mary Anne became Mrs Walker in the Church of England, married by a Church of England clergyman, within sight of the Sandemanian Chapel which had been the chosen church of her family for a very long time, while Thomas took Mary Anne as his wife in an Anglican service which would have been very new to him. His nephew, Hector Turnbull, who was also a long-time friend, and who owned a calenderer's factory in St Andrews Street, Dundee, served as best man at the ceremony. Thomas's daughter Grace also signed the certificate as witness, whilst Mary Anne's sister Elizabeth and brother Oswald did the same.

The Walker side of Mary Lily's family were firmly rooted in Dundee. Her great-grandfather, John, was an important trader and businessman, and, residing as he did in Dundee's Murraygate, he would have had a number of the town's most prominent people as neighbours. He was also a burgess of the town, a distinction which meant he was amongst the social and economic elite; less than a tenth of the men in Dundee were burgesses. John was admitted as a burgess in September 1753 and this was allowed him through the right of his wife, Elizabeth Blair, who was daughter of James Blair, a glover, who himself had been admitted as a burgess in 1718. William Walker was subsequently admitted as a burgess in October 1781, by right of his father, and Thomas became a burgess of Dundee in October 1818, again through the right of his father. The Glasite Church and the Church of Scotland's St Andrews Church shared the same area, and both were within a very short walking distance of Murraygate. The Office of Boxmaster tended to be handed down within families, and John's privileged position within the Glover's Guild may well reflect that his own father had the honour before him, and he may well have worked as a glover. He must have been a well-to-do character, given that his son, William, trained to become a writer, not a glover.[53]

The population of Dundee had grown markedly in the second half of the eighteenth century. The estimated population in 1766 was around 12,400 but by 1809 there were reckoned to be around '30,000 souls'. In the same year, William Walker was one of fourteen writers in Dundee and his office was at the top of Castle Street at its junction with the High Street. His son, Thomas, was 11 years of age in 1809, and he was one of ten children to William and his wife, Jane Livingston. Jane was Mary Lily's grandmother and she bore ten children between the years of 1787 and 1804. Thomas was the seventh of these children and he would outlive all the others. The family were living in a town that changed shape as its population grew. Castle Street and Crichton Street were recent additions to the town's map, allowing much better and much wider access from the High Street to the shore and docks area. Tay Street, at the top of the recently broadened Nethergate, was a very wide street joining the West Port to the junction of the Nethergate and Perth Road. The Dundee directories of the period hint at a real sense of civic pride as the town updates and grows, but with these new streets, and the new buildings springing up along them, came the problems of fresh water provision and of waste collection.[54]

The responsibility for these problems was vested in the police force. They controlled sanitary arrangements, the list of regulations, and issued the subsequent fines for *'transgressors'*, which reveal that some people in Dundee were not very careful with household and human waste. For example, no one was allowed to deposit on the streets *'foul water, ashes or any filth whatever'* between the hours of six in the morning and eight in the evening and the penalty for non-compliance was 1 shilling for the first offence and 2 shillings and sixpence for further transgressions. Everyone was *'expressly debarred'* from dumping *'any filth or nastiness'* on Saturday nights, because the scavengers did not work on that evening. After seven in the morning (after nine in winter) any person *'shaking carpets, floor-cloths, bed-curtains, or cloths of any kind, over windows, doors or stairs'* would be fined two shillings and sixpence. The same fine applied to first-time offenders if they threw waste and *'nuisances'* out of doors or windows onto the street. A worse transgression still was the *'keeping of dung in closes'*, which carried a 5-shilling penalty, and dung deposited onto the streets had to be removed by the *'stablers or cow-feeders'* by seven in the morning or else they would be fined *'10s. Sterling'*.

The dearth of sewerage provision in Dundee, and the absence of any running water into businesses and households, was something that would not be adequately addressed almost until Thomas's death in 1876; the Dundee that Thomas knew and lived in faced a constant battle over housing provision for its rapidly growing population and the problems of the increasingly heavy demand on its water supply and its waste disposal. The prospect of going to church on a Sunday probably cleansed souls if not streets, and it was almost certainly through his Glasite Church that Thomas met his first wife.

Catherine Sandeman Morison was born in Perth in 1800. Her parentage linked her to two of the most prominent families in Perth. The Sandemans owned the bleach-works at Luncarty in Perthshire, in partnership with the Turnbulls. Robert Sandeman, who was the son-in-law of John Glas, was one of her uncles. The Turnbulls and the Sandemans were linked by more than business. Hector Turnbull (1733–1788) was the grandfather to the Hector Turnbull who was Thomas Walker's best man. The older Hector married another of John Glas's daughters, Agnes, who bore him four children in four years before she died in April 1761. He married again in October that year. His new wife Mary Walker was the sister of John Walker of Dundee (Thomas's grandfather). Hector and Mary then had a recorded sixteen children, and five of their children married five of his partner William Sandeman's children. All were members in the Glasite Church in Perth where the marriage ceremonies took place. Thomas Walker's first wife, Catherine, was therefore a distant cousin of her husband, but she had Morison blood in her veins too.

The Morisons were traders and commercial accountants in Perth, and the men of the family had a tradition of being members of The Society of High Constables of the City of Perth. The connections between the two Glasite chapels, and their congregations in Perth and Dundee, was particularly strong, and Catherine's family would have encouraged her interest in the young man from Dundee with such good professional prospects and from such a prominent and Glasite family.

They were married in Thomas's hometown of Dundee on the 13th July 1820, and the first of their eight children, who was named Anna Louisa after Catherine's mother, was born on 13th February 1822. Sadly, Anna Louisa appears to have had some sort of mental illness, which resulted in her being put to Gartnavel Asylum, near Glasgow, for a while. This would have been after 1843, when the Glasgow Lunatic Asylum, sited where the present day Buchanan Street Bus Station sits, relocated to new premises away from the hubbub and pollution of the city. When Montrose Asylum moved to much improved premises in 1858, Anna Louisa Walker seems to have moved there. In 1871 she boarded with Mrs Elizabeth Ramsay, at Craig, to the south of Montrose. Ramsay had previously worked at the asylum. On his death, in Thomas's bequests to his *'beloved'* children, Anna's inheritance was to be administered by a Factor. Anna Louisa Walker was two years older than her stepmother when Thomas married for the second time.

Mary Lily had three half-sisters; only Anna Louisa, Eliza and Grace were still living from the children of his first marriage. Thomas's first wife, Catherine, had died of consumption in 1835, by which time Grace, the youngest of her children, was under three years of age. Catherine was not a blood relation of Mary Lily, but Eliza and Grace would have presumably told her about their mother, and would almost certainly have taken her along to the Howff to see the gravestone that memorialised their grandparents and mother and their five deceased siblings. The gravestone sits adjacent to that of the Rev John Glas; a reminder of how close the Walker family were, and remained, to the founder of their Church.

Eliza Walker was only four years younger than her father's new wife. She did not sign the marriage certificate for the Kirkby Lonsdale wedding, whilst younger sister Grace did. Protocol in Victorian times was very strong, and had Eliza been at the wedding she would certainly have been the signatory before her sister. The 1861 census reveals that Eliza was living in the family home at 152 Perth Road, but ten years later, in 1871, she is not recorded in any Dundee or Angus location; nor was she residing with her sister Anna Louisa. Eliza may well have gone to some other relatives for a while, but her apparent non-appearance at her father's wedding, and her move away from the family home, might perhaps signal a rift of some sort. Grace, who is fully ten years younger than her stepmother, appears to have accepted her father's decision, and she is ever present in all of the census returns of the family.

Mary Lily's presence would have been very novel for Grace. Being the youngest of Thomas's first family, she would have had no exposure to babies in the house until Lily, and it is easy to imagine that she would have delighted in the experience. With Magadalen Green on their doorstep, Grace would almost certainly have pushed her younger sister in her pushchair along to the new park where cricket and bowls were played on sunny days, and where trains could be viewed puffing their way to and from Perth. Sundays may well have been days of partial separation though. Mary Anne was a member of the Church of England, and became a member of the recently opened Scottish Episcopal Church of St Paul, situated at the top of Seagate on Castle Hill. Grace and Eliza were both long-time members of the Free Church of St Peters, a church that was built in 1836 and was situated on the opposite side of the road from the family home when they stayed on the Perth Road. There is little record of Mary Lily's early church days, but she was a member of the Episcopal Church in her university days, and it seems logical to presume that Mary Anne would have taken her daughter to her own church. This is borne out by the fact that Mary Lily's younger brother, Arthur, attended Glenalmond College in Perthshire as a boarder, and Glenalmond at that time was a school for the children of people from the Scottish Episcopalian faith. Thomas's dilemma would have been in whether to attend church with his wife, or the Free Church of his daughters Eliza and Grace, or he might have felt obliged to attend St Andrew's Church, where he acted as Boxmaster to the Glovers. It may well have been the last of these options that he took, partly because he would not be choosing between family commitments, and partly to cement professional and commercial interests. St Andrews, with its adjacent burial ground, was a very popular site for the exchange of talk between Dundee's business elite at the time.

Further "proof" of Thomas's allegiance and duty to St Andrews can be found in a stained glass window in the Church, entitled, The Walker Window. This window is to the east/front of the church and it depicts the Good Shepherd finding his lost sheep. The following inscription attends the window:

Erected by his family in memory of Thomas Walker,
Notary Public, Dundee the first Scottish lawyer
who appealed from the Supreme Court in Edinburgh to
the House of Lords.
Obit: February, 1876.
This window is by Mayer and Company – Munich & London.

Mary Lily Walker commissioned this tribute to her beloved father. She had been 12 when he died, and the last three years of his life would have seen his dementia steadily worsen. He died at home, in Sunnybank, where his doctor, J M Miller, certified the death. The person who registered the event was his business partner, John Duff Bruce, who lived at 4 Fords Lane at the time, although he had not been present at the death. The doctor listed the causes as bronchitis, which Thomas had apparently suffered from for two months, and *'softening of the brain'*. In Scotland at this time, deaths had to be registered within seven days; Thomas's was registered in two. It was then the task of the Registrar to contact the doctor concerned to confirm the cause of death. This was duly completed and Thomas was laid to rest beside his sisters at Western Cemetery.

Arthur, Mary Lily's younger brother, became the "man of the house" at Sunnybank until John Duff Bruce assumed the position after marrying Eliza. By the time he died, Thomas would have known that his youngest daughter was very intelligent, and that she was thriving at school, but his mental condition would have meant that he was not aware of how academically bright his son would be. Had he lived longer, he may have become worried by his son's social skills.

Chapter 3

Lighting the Flame

Mary Lily's first school is not recorded, though it may well have been Dundee High School where her father had been a subscribing director since 1864. From the age of 10 she attended a newly opened school, Tayside House, which was located at 162 Nethergate, Dundee. This *'Select Private School and Boarding Establishment'* began its tenure as a teaching establishment in 1873. It accepted girls as boarders or as day students, and also taught boys up to the age of 12.[55]

The 1872 Education Act meant that it became compulsory for all children between 5 and 13 to have schooling and it also opened the way for more women to enter the teaching profession. Miss Sarah Cannon Buchan ran Tayside House from its outset and offered classes in English, Latin, French, German and Italian, and also in Science, Arithmetic, Algebra and Mathematics. Lessons were also taught in more practical subjects such as Needlework, Writing, Drawing, Music (which comprised of Piano, Violin and Singing), Drill, Dancing and Callisthenics. The school took pride in preparing pupils for University entry examinations, something that was prompted by connections to St Andrews University, though Miss Buchan would have known about the increasing likelihood of Dundee having its own University College.

Miss Buchan devoted herself to teaching, along with a number of other female and male teachers. The school cited academic connections to J.M.D. Meiklejohn, the Professor of Education at St Andrews University, and to the same establishment's Professor of Humanities, the Rev. Alex Roberts. This seems to have been a good enough school in which to be taught, and Mary Lily would prove herself to be a gifted pupil.

The 1886 prospectus for the school, which detailed the subjects to be covered in the fourteenth year since its opening, lists the University College Principal, Professor William Peterson, as a referee, and his brother, Magnus, as the piano teacher. The proximity of the school to the new further education establishment (being directly across the road) would have meant that the eyes of Tayside House pupils were drawn to the College.

Tayside House provided Mary Lily with her education until she was 16. She then attended Dundee High School for two further years of learning. During this period, Mary Lily displayed her academic abilities by winning several school prizes. In 1880 she won four separate awards in French, German, Perspective and Practical Geometry, and the following year she won the fourth-year Senior School prize for French.

During her time at Tayside House, a lot of building and development work was taking place in Dundee. The school building was a large detached Georgian townhouse but, almost as soon as it opened, work began on the building of the Queens Hotel, which would abut the school to the town side. The Queens Hotel was originally to be called the Station Hotel, in readiness for the rail links which were mooted to be terminating at the door, but the change of plans by the railways meant a change of name.[56] Owned by a consortium of local businessmen, the Queens Hotel was fronted by a man who called himself Col Smith. He had owned The Vaults pub in Dundee around 1865, where he did particularly well, and he would go on to be the sole agent in the area for the prestigious beer making company, Messrs Bass & Co from Burton-on-Trent. The Queens Hotel was a worry for him when it opened because it seemed to be in the wrong location. After His Royal Highness the King of Saxony stayed there with his entourage, however, the hotel became the place to stay for nobility and distinguished visitors to Dundee.

The noise during the construction of the hotel may have been very disruptive to school lessons, and to the back of the school was the Seabraes Spinning Mill, owned by J & A Guthrie. This large mill sat on ground between the Caledonian Railway's line to Perth and the town's Perth Road. The din of the mill and the railway carriages rumbling along tracks would also have been audible for the pupils. Mary Lily walked to school from the family home in Magdalen Yard Road. From the large town-house that the Walker family had moved to in the mid-1860s, it would have taken no more than ten minutes to complete her daily journey. She would have passed the Tay Rope Works which, at 51 Magdalen Yard Road, was less than two hundred yards from her home. This narrow building stretched up towards the Perth Road behind, and it was considered a blight to the eye next to the lovely properties of Roseangle and Magdalen Green.[57] But Dundee had a well-deserved reputation for permitting commercial enterprises to be sited amongst grand middle-class houses and shops.[58] The steady climb up Roseangle towards the Perth Road would have interested Mary Lily. Houses of all shapes and sizes were springing up around this period and this street had its share of variety and grandeur. [59]

Before she had turned up Roseangle, her eyes and ears would have been fixed on the construction that was taking shape at the side of the Tay. This was the beginning of the Tay Railway

Bridge, and from the upstairs window of her home Mary Lily, and no doubt the rest of the family, would watch the progress of this wonder unfold. Wormit, across the river, would have been fully visible to the residents at Sunnybank, but, at almost two miles distant, it must have seemed an enormous expanse over which to place a bridge. The whole town knew that this was a world news event; the longest metal construction to be built in history, and in the four years from her starting at Tayside House until its completion in 1877, the sight of the Tay Railway Bridge must have captured Mary Lily's interest. She might have witnessed the first workman's engine crossing the bridge on 22nd September 1877, and heard of the first passenger crossing in early June 1878.

She would have heard about United States President, Ulysses Simpson Grant, when he came to see the *'mighty big bridge for such a small city'*. Grant arrived, and left, to little ceremony, on 1st September 1877. He had asked for *'no fuss'*, though the public in Dundee did turn out in great numbers to witness the *'stout, little, unassuming gentleman in the blue coat'* as he took the trip in a carriage along Magdalen Yard Road towards the *'greatest railway bridge in the world'*.[60] She would know, too, about the visit of the Emperor of Brazil, who arrived with Count de Lamaire, and Chevalier de Macedo, on the morning of 3rd July 1877. *'Several thousands of a crowd'* awaited them. The Emperor arrived by train and was taken by horse-drawn carriage up Union Street, along Nethergate, and down Roseangle to Magdalen Green. The carriage may have pulled up almost exactly outside Mary Lily's house, where the distinguished visitors *'walked over the green to the bridge, taking time to pat a small boy, perched at the front of the onlookers, on the head'*.[61] The appearance of such world-renowned visitors (Prince Leopold of Belgium was another who visited) prompted the call that the Tay Bridge should be considered the *'eighth wonder of the world'* and the *Courier* went further by considering it to be *'a little more wonderful than some of the venerable seven'*. The phrase "pride comes before a fall" had rarely been more accurately or aptly made, given that the structure would collapse in little more than two years.[62]

People were permitted to walk on the bridge on the 22nd September 1877, as far out as the northern edge of the highest girders. Countless people took the opportunity to witness, at very close quarters, the first train across. The little works engine, *The Mongrel*, had the distinction of pulling a couple of carriages across, and it was held up on two occasions because of the people flooding the track. As it rounded the curve at the Dundee end, a passenger train from Perth passed simultaneously, with its entire compliment of passengers waving excitedly at the sight. Lily may have been watching this historic event, and she may also have watched as Queen Victoria travelled south over the bridge in June 1879. The Queen clearly liked looking at Dundee more than she liked staying in it, and she was noted to have once said, *'the situation of the town is very fine, but the town itself is not so '*.[63]

Mary Lily's thoughts of the bridge would have evaporated by the time she had left Rosangle and gained the flat section of Perth Road. She would first walk past a few older buildings, flatted tenements of three stories, with no running water, and no sanitary arrangements other than the scavengers who attended to the discarded waste. A different sight would capture her attention just a little further on; here she would walk past some newly built tenement blocks. In a few yards, Lily would be seeing the past and the future buildings of Dundee, and the change in water and sewage provision. The new buildings had been connected to the new sewage system – forty-six miles of underground pipes leading to the Tay which was causing so many roads to be dug and re-dug as it slowly inched its way around the main streets of the town. The Improvement Act of 1871 demanded, too, that water provision in Dundee must be radically improved. There had been The Dundee Water Act of 1845, but, to the chagrin of the council, this resulted in improved returns on private investment rather than an improved water supply. Further Water Acts in the early 1870s did, however, bring great benefits in reservoir capacity, with the new facility at Clatto adding to the greatly increased water level at Lintrathen.[64]

These buildings also housed a few new shops at ground level, and Lily would pass the undertaker's premises of J & J Gray. This company also sold furniture and Venetian blinds, built in premises in nearby Seabraes. By looking down Perth Road from their "double-doored" shop front, she could see the school where she would feed her appetite for learning and excel in academic pursuits, and across the road were the row of four townhouses that would eventually form the initial substance of University College.

When Lily was 5 years old, her father was 70 years of age, and by the time his daughter first attended Tayside House, Thomas Walker was beginning to show early signs of dementia. He began to wind down from his heavy workload, resigning as Factor from a few positions and allowing his new business partner, John Duff Bruce, to increasingly take over his mantle. An example of this can be found in the minutes of a meeting of the Governors of the mortification created by the late James Guthrie of Ardgaith. This mortification was for the benefit of the charitable institution known as 'The Home', located in Paton's Lane where Mary Lily's mother had been on the Ladies Committee. Thomas resigned as Factor in January 1874. Such was their regard for his services that the Governors were moved to write:

*In accepting the resignation of Mr Walker the Meeting
desired to express the great pleasure they had had in all*

their communications with him during the whole period of his management as Factor, and they desired the new Factor (John Duff Bruce) to transmit to Mr Walker an excerpt from this minute.

Thomas Walker, who had fathered ten children, and had been a prominent solicitor for his entire working life, died at the advanced age of 78 years on February 24th 1876. He had lived longer than five of his children and all of his siblings. He was buried in Dundee's Western Cemetery in the same lair as his two older sisters: Jean, who had died on the 8th of January 1862, and Elizabeth, who died on the 8th of August 1864. The cause of his death was said to have been from *'softening of the brain'*, from which he had apparently suffered for over three years.[65] It is probable that this progressively worsening mental state was related to Alzheimer's disease, a condition which would explain his gradual departure from the profession he loved and from the several committees and organisations for which he did sterling service. This would, of course, include his role as Boxmaster to the Glovers Guild, a position he took pride in holding, and which his father and grandfather had held before him.

He had witnessed much change in the town of Dundee. His family was an old Dundee family, and the family links and business friendships would have meant that Thomas was a well-known figure. He had been listed in the Dundee Postal Directory as a writer in 1824, which, given he was born in 1798, meant that he achieved this status at a very early age. There were less than 20,000 inhabitants in Dundee when he was born, but this had grown to well over 120,000 by the time he retired. Whilst Thomas had watched this enormous growth in the population of his hometown, he would also have witnessed the great social changes that swept the nation. Signs of the drive towards industrialisation were evident in the chimneys that stood out in the skyline all around him, and the noisy factories and foundries that seemed to spring up so readily. The constant incoming of new faces and different dialects, even different languages, must have had him wondering where it would end. With these immigrants came new churches, different customs and overcrowding, which brought with it illnesses and filth.

Social habits were being challenged, and being changed too. Women in Dundee, especially in the textile industries based around the manufacture of linen and jute products, were populating the workplace in a way that was so different from Thomas's younger days, and with this influx of industrial labour came a propensity to drinking. He may well have been surprised by the number of women who also partook in this *'regrettable activity'*.[66] By all accounts, Thomas Walker was a reputable, hard-working and successful business professional, and his main concern in life was in providing for the welfare of his children. When Mary Lily came along, Thomas might have realised the growing importance of education for girls in a way that he may not have appreciated before. Mary Lily's bright intelligence shone early, and he would have known of the probability of Dundee, through its wealthy elite, planning to open a further-education facility of sorts, but the likelihood of Mary Lily being able to attend such an establishment would not have been considered in the mid-1870s. Thomas Walker would have died expecting his dutiful, intelligent, 13-year-old daughter, Mary Lily, to join with her half-sisters in doing good and charitable works. At this period in Scottish history, however, a lot happened in a short time.

Lily may have been ignorant and naïve of the squalid areas of town due to her sheltered upbringing, but her ignorance of the world stretched only so far. She was a reasonably regular visitor to her uncle's house in Kendal, and to his draper's shop there too, no doubt. The sights and sounds and the smells on the train journey to Kendal and back would have been very different from the odorous air of Dundee, and the trip would have necessitated a change of trains in Glasgow, possibly even an overnight stay in Scotland's biggest city. These trips were undertaken with her mother, and became less frequent as Mary Anne became more infirm. One trip down to England, though, was more memorable than the rest.

This trip was to a wedding, held on the 26th of June 1878. Mary Lily Walker, at the age of 15, was to be bridesmaid to her half-sister, Eliza, and as Eliza was the only one of Thomas's ten children ever to marry, this must have been a very exciting prospect. Grace was the other bridesmaid, and it is easy to imagine the railway journey to the wedding being one of huge excitement and anticipation. Eliza was marrying her father's business partner, John Duff Bruce. The happiness of the day may well have been slightly dampened by the fact that Thomas Walker had died two years earlier.

The wedding was a curious affair for a few reasons. For one thing, at 50, Eliza was six years older than her husband. This was not at all unheard of in Victorian times, but it was unusual to have such a gap when the woman was the older partner. The couple chose to be married in a Church of England service, yet both Eliza and John were members of the Free Church of Scotland, and they regularly attended the Church of St Peter, situated in Dundee's Perth Road. The Church of England required banns to be read out, each Sunday, in the three weeks before the marriage in the home church of each of the parties, and in the church where the marriage was to take place. Whether this happened in the case of Eliza and John is unknown, though it could have been circumvented if a Bishop's certificate was arranged. The wedding took place in the Church of St John the Divine, in Lytham, Lancashire, and was conducted by the Rev Evan Williams. His church was situated on the East Beach at Lytham, and at that time it had an undisturbed view of the sea.

Why the couple would have decided on a wedding at this venue, in a church that was not of their denomination and so far from home, is a matter for conjecture. Certainly it would have been close to the Allens from Kirkby Lonsdale, but then they could have opted for the very church in Kirkby Lonsdale where Thomas and Mary Allen had married some sixteen years earlier, an option more convenient to Mary Anne's family. It might simply have been that this was a perfect, romantic spot to have a wedding, being easily accessible by rail since the Kirkham to Blackpool rail line had opened the previous year. Lytham had its own promenade, and it was a peaceful, unhurried little town, so unlike the noisy bustling town of Dundee which they had temporarily left behind. It was within a few minutes of Blackpool, which was rapidly gaining a reputation for its tourist facilities, and which would hold its first ever "illumination" just a year later. The railway network had created a thirst for travel and for holiday resorts, and the speed at which rail track was covering the country was astounding. But as well as being a testament to British engineering and planning, the railway occasionally brought despair.

On the 28th December 1879, a day and night of gale force winds that howled down the estuary of the Tay, the two-year-old railway bridge came down with an engine and carriages. It was dark when the disaster took place, but within a very short time people all over the town heard about the rumour that the train from Edinburgh had plunged into the river. The commotion in the street would have brought Eliza and John Bruce to the door of their house in Magdalen Yard Road. Shortly after the marriage, Mary Lily and her mother had left Sunnybank to live in Windsor Terrace, leaving the big house for the newly wed couple and sister Grace to live in. Such was the commotion and consternation around the northern end of the railway bridge that Sunday night, which was little more than two hundred yards from Sunnybank, that word may well have reached Mary Lily and her mother. The disaster was certainly the talk of the town and the substance of local newspapers for many weeks and months, especially with each body pulled from the Tay and discovered even further away. From the rear windows of Tayside House, the pupils would have seen the tortuously mangled wreckage of the bridge, and the stumps that were the only reminder of the centre section.

Many people in Dundee would have recalled the earlier incident, on Sunday February 4th 1877, when a sudden and *'terrific'* gale blew down two of the largest girders from the nearly completed bridge. It was reported that forty men had had to spend a frightening night on the bridge because the ferocity of the wind and sea forbade any rescue attempt. *The Courier & Argus*, on the 5th February, stated that *'this may to some extent weaken the public faith in its secure stability'*. There were doubts about the possibility of such a long structure managing to withstand the tides and the winds that often affected the Tay, and some, in letters to the *Weekly News*, mentioned William McGonagall's prophetic sixth verse of his "poem" on the new bridge. For quite a long time after the collapse, although there was a body of pressure to span the Tay again with a stronger railway bridge, a sense of despondency lay over the town. However, other events were conspiring to change this.

The opening of University College in Dundee altered the character of the town, and the lives of countless people, forever. The opportunities this new place of further education offered cannot be overstated, and not just for the students who would find themselves being taught through this bold new facility.

The light of education would bring attention to the city from places and people that had never shown interest in it before. The conditions laid down for University College by Miss Mary Ann Baxter, who was substantially the main benefactor, included a plain mandate that women should, and would, be allowed exactly the same educational opportunities and experiences as men, meaning that they would be taught in the same classrooms, at the same time. This decision was groundbreaking, very enlightened, and highly controversial for the period. When Mary Lily Walker matriculated at the beginning of term in 1883, she immediately became one of the first students of this new and exciting educational establishment, but she also became one of the very first women in Scotland to be taught, and to be assessed, in the same environment, and by the same standards as male students.[67]

But Mary Lily was not the only member of the Walker household to start her university life that day: her brother Arthur, and their half-sister Grace, also enrolled for further education at Dundee. At the age of 16, Arthur was one of the youngest students, and Grace was one of the eldest at the age of 48. The fact that the location of the College was directly across the road from Tayside House, where so much of her formative learning had taken place, would also have been seen as a great benefit. By 1883 Mary Lily was looking after her mother, Mary Anne, who had become an invalid, and the option to undertake further education in some of the other Scottish universities was not one she would have considered. She was living at 10 Airlie Place with her brother and mother; a house which was very close to the four townhouses that had been linked together to form University College. Also living in Airlie Place was a girl of the same age named Margaret (Meta, as she was better known) Peterson. She was a younger sister of the first University College Principal, William Peterson, and was to become a fellow student and lifelong close friend to Mary Lily. Mary Lily was fortunate that the college opened at exactly the time that best suited her needs, but she was also fortunate in the professors and tutors who were teaching at this new educational establishment.

William Peterson was just 26 when he was chosen, ahead of 42 others, for the post of Principal. He was a classical scholar and took on the Chair of Classics with Ancient History at University College, Dundee. The Chair of Natural Philosophy and Mathematics was given to another very young man, J.E.A. Stegall, who had been one of the unsuccessful candidates for the role as Principal, and whom Mary Lily would get to know very well through the Dundee Social Union (DSU). The first Professor of Chemistry, Thomas Carnelley, was older, but still only 30. He would be very actively involved with the DSU and would eventually have the Chemistry building, the first new building in the college, named after him. Due to the limited size of the building and the reasonably few day students (138), the staff and students would be in close contact with each other. Mary Lily would also have met the 27-year-old Chair of Engineering and Drawing, Alfred Ewing, who was a Dundonian, and also the *'old-man'* of the teaching fraternity, the 31-year-old Chair of English and Modern History, Thomas Gilray.[68] On 5th October 1883, the opening ceremony was performed by Lord Dalhousie, and an auspicious day was only marred by Mary Ann Baxter's absence, which was attributed to a family bereavement. For Mary Lily Walker and new friends, this must have been an exciting, if slightly daunting, day. The *'haunting lines'* from local worthy, William McGonagall, which he penned for the inauguration, may have brought laughter mixed with trepidation:

*I hope the ladies and gentlemen of Dundee will try and learn knowledge
At home in Dundee in their nice little College,*

Because knowledge is sweeter than honey or jam,
Therefore let them try and gain knowledge as quick as
they can.[69]

Two years after her first day at college, Mary Lily would meet the youngest of all the Chairs when D'Arcy Wentworth Thompson arrived to take up his place in Biology. At the age of 24, when he accepted the post, Thompson was less than three years older than Lily, and in this man she would find an excellent tutor and a brilliant scientist who would become a lifelong friend. When Patrick Geddes joined the ranks in 1888, accepting the Chair of Botany, he was 34, and his arrival made even brighter the constellation of shining young talents tutoring in the new college.[70]

Mary Lily Walker's time at University College was a successful one by any standards. In 1886–87 she won the Botany Prize, and another for Advanced Latin, whilst her friends, Meta Peterson and Etta Johnston, won prizes for Analytical Classes, Comparative Anatomy and Embryology between them. In 1887–88 Lily lifted the prizes for Embryology, Zoology and Physiology, whilst Etta took the Chemistry prize and Meta the General Biology. In the early days, these prize-giving events were held publicly. Mary Lily matriculated every year from 1883 to 1894, and sometimes helped in teaching new students as her own experience grew. These were heady days for Mary Lily and her fellow female students who were not only relishing the unique experience that University College was affording them, but were competing on equal terms with male students and regularly outperforming them. Mary Lily and her brother even attended the Saturday Day Classes that the college ran, and in 1890–91 Mary won the Physiology prize again.

Her progress, and that of her peers, would have been recognised by the professors and lecturers, especially by D'Arcy Thompson who would, much later, look back on her days at the college with the following recollection:

Mary Lily Walker was a student of mine soon after I came to Dundee, a young woman like many another, of the simplest, homeliest upbringing, of scanty opportunities, devoted to an invalid mother, knowing little or nothing of the world. She was an excellent student; she learned a great deal of Natural History. I remember telling her as I handed her her medal that there had not been a single word in her exam paper from beginning to end which I could have altered and improved.[71]

This period in Mary Lily's life was as close to self-indulgence as she was ever to get. She thrived in the atmosphere of university education, and she gained friends not only amongst her fellow students, but also amongst the academic professionals who formed that early idyll. This friendship and respect carried beyond the classroom when she became interested in a venture that was being started by the staff. The Dundee Social Union became the platform from which Mary Lily's journey into social reform would begin. Whilst her mother and her sisters had busied themselves for years serving on many good-cause committees for destitute women, orphan children, for the Young Women's Christian Association and for Dundee Industrial Schools, Mary Lily had contented herself in gaining as good an education as she could. The opportunity to contribute to DSU gave her the chance to follow the praiseworthy efforts of her relatives in a very positive way. Life for Mary Lily would change forever, and would bring her into direct contact with the poorest and most deprived people in the town.

Chapter 4

Scaling the Heights

The 1880s and 90s were not good times to be born in Dundee, unless you were born in the right part of the city. The impact of the Improvement Act of 1871 had not yet reached most of the dire and desperate slum areas where the vast majority of Dundee's workforce dwelt. Housing, already vastly overcrowded, became even worse as flats and properties were sub-divided to accommodate the ever-increasing demand. Infant mortality was shocking: two in every five children died before they reached their first birthdays, and worse, four out of every five children born in those most unsanitary of conditions died before they reached the age of 3.[72] Infanticide was sometimes the cause. Mothers and fathers who simply could not feed another mouth, or squeeze in another body, lay on their babies to extinguish life that had no hope. It was almost considered a kindness by many.[73] Illness and disease also impacted on this heinous death rate, but this could hardly be otherwise given the prevailing conditions and the lack of sanitary provision. Living in these conditions was to live a life of hardship. The well-intentioned housewife could do her best to keep a well swept and tidy home, but all around was squalor, and poverty, and the mood was mostly of despondency. To be poor in Dundee at this time was extremely common, and the spirit of hope seemed starkly uncommon.

Dundee Social Union was formed at University College Dundee by a group of professional people who felt they simply had to do something to help the very poorest citizens of Dundee. The sight of the blighted children and adults was never far from their view, particularly just to the north of the college. D'Arcy Thomson, looking back on the early days of his time in Dundee, remembered:

> *Dundee was terribly poor. When I first came here the Greenmarket was full of idle men, walking to and fro, hungry and in rags. Of all those young professors who had just come to the town, I doubt if there was one who was not shocked and saddened by the poverty which Dundee openly displayed.*[74]

Professor J A Ewing, who was the son of a Dundee church minister, founded a Sanitary Association which he set up to investigate the condition in which the poorest lived. This followed an earlier experiment by Thomas Carnelley, who, with the able assistance of John Haldane, an old school-fellow of Darcy Thompson's, *'wanted to study the foul air of the overcrowded dwellings in the light of the new germ-theory of disease'*. The pair, accompanied by a policeman, went from crowded house to crowded house capturing the fetid air in a jelly-filled tube on which the cultures and colonies grew. Despite carrying out this task on a large number of occasions, they never failed to feel devastated at the dreadful conditions. D'Arcy went with them once or twice and reported that *'what I saw I have never forgotten'*.[75]

Carnelley and Haldane had the backing of A M Anderson, who was Dundee's Medical Officer for Health at the time. Thomas Kinnear, who headed the town's Sanitary Department, gave them a horse-drawn covered wagon. This wagon was used to aid the collection and analysis of samples. As well as the policeman, two inspectors from the Sanitary Department often accompanied the scientists. The element of surprise was crucial, as any kind of advance warning might result in houses and rooms being ventilated which would effectively make the results untypical. Night visits were the norm because it was then that the greatest degree of overcrowding existed, and that fresh air was excluded and ventilation shut down.[76] Carnelley found that the air quality in the inspected homes was often at least five times worse than was deemed tolerable.

Being woken in the middle of the night by a group of scientists, sanitary officers and a policeman can hardly have been a welcome intrusion for the inhabitants of the chosen houses. Word would have quickly spread that this was happening, but it must still have been traumatic and probably embarrassing for the tenants. However, the prospect of conditions being improved by these incursions must have been enough to gain tacit approval, as there were relatively few complaints and even fewer signs of aggression from those who were knocked upon.

Ewing's Sanitary Association led to the formation of DSU in 1888, and Professors Thomas Carnelley, George Ogilvie and J E A Stegall joined Ewing in the enterprise. D'Arcy Thompson joined soon afterwards. Patrick Geddes was not amongst the group, presumably because it had been formed only a matter of weeks after his arrival in Dundee, but, having been involved in the Edinburgh Social Union, it is probable that he played some sort of advisory role at the very least.[77] The ethos of the Union was to

> *improve the surroundings and lives of the poor in direct and indirect ways; one of the most tangible methods is thought to be the superintendence of their dwellings with a view to their repair and enlargement, and their cleanly and healthful condition.*

This was a lofty and ambitious aim, and it would rely heavily on the work of those engaged in visiting the houses of the poor and gaining their confidence and co-operation.

The first meeting of the Dundee Social Union was on the 24th May 1888, where the rules and regulations, as well as the main aims, were thrashed out. The basic intention was to improve the housing conditions of the poor, and to provide *'opportunities and to cultivate a taste for healthy enjoyments'*. Three main committees were formed at this point, the first being in charge of Housing, the second was a Sanitary Committee, and the third looked to draw up a programme of activities in their capacity as the Arts and Recreation Committee. Helping people to help themselves was the war-cry, but enabling them to work for the common good at the same time was the higher aspiration. Two housing superintendents, Miss Gourley and Miss Hill, were soon appointed, and their remit was the day-to-day management of properties that the DSU would purchase and rent out. These owned properties were four slum tenement blocks, the first three of which were in Bell Street, Watson's Lane and Union Street in Maxwelltown. These were in three quite different areas of the town: Bell Street was very near the centre, whilst Watson's Lane was off the Hawkhill towards the west of town, and Union Street, Maxwelltown, was to the north of town. All three suffered desperately poor conditions. Each was sited close to the mills and factories that produced the textile products on which the economy, and a huge percentage of the workforce, so depended. This was how it had to be in Dundee; with the long hours worked, and the feeding of families and looking after of houses, the shorter the trip to work the better. To be offering a mill worker housing of better quality more distant from their workplace was offering them nothing useful.

Union Street, Maxwelltown, not to be confused with the wide thoroughfare leading from Nethergate which was opened in 1828, was famous for a very different yet equally tragic reason. The Tay Railway disaster claimed the lives of two unrelated men from that very street when George Taylor, a mason who lived at No 56, and William Threlfell, a confectioner from

No 9, were reported lost. When the DSU took ownership of this property, their collectors would probably hear of this singular misfortune which had visited their street in 1879 many times.

In managing and collecting restricted rents as landlords, the DSU put in strict rules of conduct. The lady rent-collectors, furnished with pencil and rent book, were to go round their allotted pitch, and were encouraged to engage in day-to-day talk with tenants as they collected rent. Thereafter the monies and rent book, duly marked to indicate those who had paid and those who had not, were handed over to the superintendent, and issues like building repairs were then discussed and hopefully implemented. Around seventy families lived in these properties and the conditions in which they lived at the time the DSU took them over, were considered representative of conditions in most of the worst parts of Dundee.[78] One of the academic group, Professor Franklin, played a relatively little part in the DSU, but when he departed from Dundee he left a significant sum of money to help the work of the Union. He was not a particularly wealthy man, but he was profoundly moved by the depth of poverty in the city. His money would no doubt have been most welcome to the Union, but an even more valuable addition to the ranks came in the shape of one of the students.

Mary Lily Walker studied subjects under Stegall, Ewing and D'Arcy Thomson, and after five years of study would have been a friend to all three. She joined the "cause" and was soon considered 'one of its most eager helpers'. From this point in her life she began to reveal an inner strength, a sense of dogged resourcefulness, and a compassion for the task in hand. This verve and work ethic was exactly what the DSU needed, and it would have inspired others to do the same. She was initially involved in the capacity of rent collector and this role would have been mentally and physically taxing. Going into the houses of some of the tenants meant seeing, hearing and smelling a world that is, nowadays, difficult to describe. Some of the houses that Mary Lily visited had no sanitary provision of any kind, whilst some would have a facility that only men would use. The pail or pails that were used every day for human waste and rubbish would legally have to be confined indoors until nightfall, and in a two-roomed house with several tenants it would have been extremely difficult or impossible to conceal them.[79]

The rent collectors did their calling on Saturday afternoons. It was as well that Sunday was not the allotted day, as the pails were not put out on a Saturday night (even the scavengers needed a day off). Saturday was a day when the mother of the house could be expected to be at home, for how else could the woman of the house, after her week's work, do her washing and cleaning and cooking? Mary Lily described this scene in the Tenth Annual Report of the DSU in 1897 with the following words:

> *The most ardent enthusiast would find it discouraging to discourse on ventilation, on a Saturday afternoon with Tommy scrubbing his face at the sink, Jeanie blacking the grate, the harassed mother with baby wrapped in her shawl, evidently eager to get off to her shopping, and the father of the family, the only one who can take life easily, reading his paper, or perhaps stretched out on the bed.*

This gentle tirade speaks volumes about the social expectancies and gender divides in the town. The work of the woman, according to Lily, never ended, while the man of the house, who may or may not be in employment, is "entitled" to his afternoon of rest and relaxation. Dundee is often afforded the nomenclature of being a woman's town, but this phrase comes with several connotations.

D'Arcy Thomson, whilst viewing Lily as one of his *'best ever students'*, felt strongly that social work was entirely suited to her sensibilities and her sense of Christian ideals. Like her mother, she was a member of the Episcopal Church of St Pauls, and her strong sense of personal responsibility, and Christian compassion, would certainly be fuelled by those shared beliefs. However, from around 1885 until 1894 she was prone to missing some Sunday sessions at the Church, a factor which the then rector, the Rev Gough, disapproved of, and which compelled Lily to describe herself in letters to D'Arcy Thompson as a *'wicked lapsed mass'*.[80] Mary Lily was to write hundreds of letters to him during her lifetime, and he did the same for her. Her faith would be dented and heightened at various times during her life, but those early days in rent-collecting, and the sights she saw, must have given her conflicting feelings in that respect. Her friend and mentor, D'Arcy, had his own views on religion, which would have been influenced by his interest and expertise in his scientific inquiries. This is reflected in a passage from one of his papers when he wrote

> *I know, or I think I know, that there are only two resurrections in the world; that of the things that sleep in the night and awaken in the day; and that of the things that perish with the winter and live again in the spring.*[81]

Mary Lily clearly retained her faith, but the depth of her conviction waxed and waned during this time of her life. She found learning, and education, to be invigorating and taxing, fascinating and rewarding, but her role with the DSU gave her a sense of real purpose that was incredibly strong. The ability to empathise with those who were utterly helpless in their spiral of unemployment, and starvation, and overcrowding and ill health, was something that gave her drive and energy, and Lily attacked the position with zeal. Only one thing blighted this new found calling, and that was the health of her mother, Mary Anne.[82]

At just what stage in her life Mary Anne became an invalid is unclear, though her death certificate does mention a debilitating heart condition that stretched back beyond five years. She died on the morning of 22nd January 1889 at 65 years of age, and so her incapacity must have at least been worsening since her daughter began her university life. Meta Peterson, Lily's dearest friend from the college, remembered the devotion of Lily as a daughter to an invalid mother as if the condition had been there all the time she knew Lily. Her funeral service was held in the Church that she had spent so many Sundays in. She was from a family of regular churchgoers, with a tradition of philanthropic ideals, and the influence she had on her daughter must not be underestimated. 'The Home' in Paton's Lane was a charitable institution that she gave much time and effort to during her spell as a lady committee member. Its Christian message was one that Mary Anne was keen to support.[83] J M Miller, whose practice was at 23 Tay Street in the town, was the doctor who attended Mary Anne and signed her death certificate; he was the same doctor who had pronounced her dear husband Thomas dead twelve years earlier.

The decision on where Mary Anne should be buried must have been one that Lily and her family deliberated on for a while. Thomas, her husband, had bought the plot in the Western Cemetery in 1860, long before he even considered his marriage to Mary Anne. The plot he paid for had space for six burials, and at the time that would have allowed for him, his two older sisters, and his three remaining daughters, to be interred together. When his second wife died there were three spaces in the plot, but now his deceased wife, four living daughters and living son made things more complicated. If Mary Anne were to be buried at Western Cemetery, it would mean that only two others could follow when they themselves died. Given the age difference between the two later children, Lily and Arthur, and the three older ones, Anna Louisa and Eliza in particular, it was probable that neither of Mary Anne's two children would end up in the same plot as either of their parents. How the compromise was arrived at is impossible to tell, but Mary Anne was not buried beside her husband, but rather in the Western Necropolis at Balgay Hill in Dundee.

Thomas Walker, who had married twice in his life, and who was the father of ten children, is not buried beside either of his spouses. The Howff, where Catherine was interred, was no longer able to accept bodies for interment after 1858, and there was a lack of space in the family plot at the Western Cemetery which meant he would not lie with Mary Anne either. The plots either side of Thomas Walker's resting place were already used by the time of Mary Anne's death, but there were still many available plots at this burial site, so it is fair to assume that the decision to inter Mary Anne at Balgay Hill must have been taken for a reason; that reason might simply have been one of aesthetics.

Dundee's Western Cemetery was, according to reports, a very well-run and immaculately tidy place. There was *'more than sufficient room between various rows of graves, and there is a sense of quiet dignity which pervades. But it has a high enclosing wall, and attractive, but somewhat forbidding gates. All this gives a strong feeling of being exactly where you are. It feels funereal and cold'*,[84] and that must be exactly as the original planners and subsequent custodians wanted it to be. It came late into the ownership of the town and the design and atmosphere has changed little, if at all, in the years since its first funeral. Balgay Hill is different. The gravestones stand on a hill, in a much more open and airy atmosphere. The part of the cemetery where Mary Anne was interred, and where Mary Lily, Arthur and Grace would eventually join her, lies on a slope with the Celtic Cross standing much more prominently than it might have been in the flatter, more contrived aspect of the Western Cemetery. The slope gives the impression that the deceased can look out over the trees and fields, down to the river and over to Gauldry and beyond to the Fife hills, and, if imagination is strong enough, down to the green pastures of Kirkby Lonsdale. Mary Lily may well have had a lot of say in the choice of this site. No other member of the Walker family had been interred on this hill, but there was much to be liked about it as a final resting place.

Mary Lily may have picked the spot, but it was certainly her brother who paid for the plot.[85] Arthur was quite unlike his sister, and seems to have spent immeasurably more time away from Dundee than in his hometown. He was boarded out in a Perthshire school, something that Mary Lily was never asked to do, and he was forever trying to live in the shadow of his very intelligent sister. His father was almost 70 when he was born, and Arthur was barely 9 when Thomas died. Arthur was deprived of a relationship with his father because of the age difference, and because of his father's worsening dementia, but whether that had any impact on Arthur's demeanour is a matter of conjecture. Arthur was there when his mother died in the house at 9 Windsor Terrace, Dundee, and he was the one who registered the death of his mother the day after she died. The registration form describes him as an inmate at the house which meant he gave it as his present address.

Arthur's life was largely a mystery. After the death of their mother there seems to have been little, or no, contact between him and Mary Lily. This must have been a distressing situation for Lily, but given the absence of his name from most of the available correspondence between Lily and her half-sisters, friends or D'Arcy Thomson, it seems very likely that the sadness that separated them may have sprung from an early age. After the funeral of their mother Mary Lily began to throw her efforts more passionately into the social reform work that now seemed to be so much her forte, whilst Arthur appears to have gone south, probably to Manchester initially. Lily received many sympathetic letters in the weeks and months before her mother passed away. These came from friends and from her half-sister Eliza. While they could not begin to assuage her grief, they must have been of comfort to her.[86] There was a sad inevitability in her mother's passing, and Mary Lily may well have found strength for the tasks ahead at DSU from the memory of her mother's attitude to life.

Lily was appointed to the role of Superintendent of Housing and Chief Manager of DSU properties in 1891, and earnestly set about organising her force of rent collectors in a more organised fashion.[87] Octavia Hill was doing so much down in London that was akin to what was happening in Dundee, and her famous *Letter to Fellow Workers* would have been known to people in social reform, as a tract was freely available in newspaper and journal reports when it was released in 1890. The message of the letter was:

> *We have made many mistakes with our alms: eaten out the heart of the independent, bolstered up the drunkard in his indulgence, subsidised wages, discouraged thrift, assumed that many of the most ordinary wants of a working man's family must be met by our wretched and intermittent doles.*[88]

It was a simple message stating that the old-fashioned notion of mid-Victorian philanthropy, where putting a coin or two into the hands of the poor and those ill-equipped to look after themselves was considered enough of a good deed, was no longer a satisfactory solution. Mary Lily was encouraged by the DSU to go to London and work with Octavia Hill. She learned so much about the practices and methods employed there, and she must have made a very favourable impression on Octavia through her keen interest, hard work and obvious intellect, because she was offered the wardenship of a new settlement being opened in London.[89]

The offer must have been flattering and highly interesting for Lily, and she was, it seems, sorely tempted to go. She discussed the role, and the permanent move, with her friend and soulmate, Meta Peterson. Meta recalled the moment when her mind was made up for her by a really odd occurrence:

> *George Eliot's 'Romola' was not a new book; it had been written five-and-twenty years before, but it was still beloved of many. Miss Walker was fond of it, and happened to open it one day at the page where Savonarola meets Romola hurrying out of Florence, fleeing from her sorrows there. The monk told the girl that Florence was her home and her soul's dwelling place. Who should fill her place if she forsook it? 'Come back my daughter', he said, 'to your own place'.*

So Mary Lily, affected by the spiritual message in that chance paragraph, decided to stay in Dundee, and to more fully occupy the place that she had not forsaken. It would take a very different and quite tragic event for her ever to be deflected again from her role with her people in her hometown.

Lily's spell with Octavia Hill in London was a time of great research and timely work on the subject of poverty. Charles Booth alerted those who would listen, and even some who wouldn't, to the depths and the breadth to which poverty affected the lives of so many, particularly in the urban areas where overcrowding and squalor had become almost ubiquitous.[90] Samuel Barnett, a Church of England vicar, who founded Toynbee Hall in London, went further down the same line. He averred that real help, and real reform required *'personal service, not money; not a cheque not a subscription written; not speeches on a platform, not a tract; not articles in Quarterly reviews; none of the old methods but personal service – **Not money, but yourselves'**.* This message hit across all former ways of viewing and tackling a need. The argument was that nothing changes by throwing money at it and walking away, or writing about it without addressing it, or lecturing on it and at it; improvement required personal involvement and time and effort. This ideal mirrored the DSU ethos, and Mary Lily Walker was passionate about pursuing this.

But Dundee was not London. Dundee's problems were couched around the employment and labour situation that was peculiar to the city. As much as they were steeped in the overcrowding and drunkenness and insanitary conditions, Dundee's problem lay in the daily existence of its women. Women, and particularly married women, made up the textile manufacturing workforce in a way, and to an extent, that occurred in no other British town. The DSU report of 1905 shows that near to three-quarters of all those involved in that trade were women. Of 40,000 who were employed in Dundee's jute and linen factories, almost 28,000 were women. The problem in collecting monies for rent that existed in Dundee, a dilemma that was not experienced nearly so much in London, or indeed any other industrial town in Britain, was trying to find the wives and mothers at home.

Octavia Hill encouraged her rent-collectors to pass the time of day with householders; to try to get familiar with their tenants and to report and arrange repairs to properties quickly in order that excuses for not maintaining cleanliness were less frequent. This was the approach that Lily and the DSU thought might be effective in Dundee, but, for two main reasons, it proved impossible to achieve. Firstly, those working in textile mills worked long hours from Monday until Friday and then again on Saturday mornings. The only available time to collect rents would have been Saturday afternoons, and chatting at this time, as well as offering advice on matters of hygiene or house management, would have meant that getting round all the houses would be difficult. Secondly, Saturday afternoons were such a busy time for women who needed this time for cooking, cleaning, and shopping. Saturday afternoon had become a time when many of the better off in Dundee would go cycling, or walking in the hills, and this included some of those who had agreed to collect rents.[91]

The number of rent-collectors dwindled in the 1890s, and, as seems ever to be the case, the "willing horses" ended up doing the lion's share of the task. This made the opportunity to *form a relationship'*, as was encouraged in Octavia Hill's London schemes, even more unlikely. The DSU factored 102 houses in 1891, and this was only one percent of the single-roomed houses in Dundee. The DSU's Recreation Committee was set up to organise activities and concerts to *'give cheer'* to their householders. The lack of interest shown by those tenants, that manifested itself in the poor turn-outs, discouraged the DSU members to such an extent that, by 1896, the Recreation Committee was disbanded.[92] During the decade from 1890 to 1900 the DSU steadily lost members. The initial excitement, and the feelings of *'offering themselves rather than money'* began to wane, and the membership numbers dropped from ninety-eight in 1892 to sixty six in 1899. As with many such ventures, once the momentum flagged, the arrest of the decline was very steep. The DSU did regain its membership, and more, due to the efforts of Mary Lily Walker, but it took the death of a friend to serve as a catalyst. The death of Madge Valentine was a tragic loss to Mary Lily.

The outcome of that later pain would be that Mary Lily, after a good deal of soul-searching, readied herself to go to London and commit herself to spending an extended period of time with a group called "the Grey Ladies" at their religious settlement house in the capital. This settlement was run under the auspices of the Anglican Church, which was the sister church to her own. She took advice from the minister at her church, the Rev Simpson of St Pauls in Dundee, who felt it wholly sensible that she should go if she earnestly wanted to come back and act for social reform. His considered opinion was that

> *Something like a discipline and training is essential, if the enthusiasm of the amateur is to be tempered with the wisdom of the professional worker.*[93]

At this time of her life, Mary Lily felt the need for spiritual sustenance, and this was something she found with the Grey Ladies. Their organisational strengths provided Mary Lily with something she had not realised she had lacked, and that was the feeling of not acting in isolation, of being part of a centre where each served and helped each other for the common good provided through social work. The support, both temporal and spiritual, and the feeling of accomplishment all came together to make the year between 1898 and May 1899 thoroughly enjoyable and very invigorating. D'Arcy Thompson visited Mary Lily once while she was there, and beheld her for the first time in her grey habit. This was the uniform that the Grey Ladies wore when they were out and about doing their work. His impression was that she suited it well, although she wrote to him about it at the time, demurring that *'the frock is, as you say, neither here or there, it is necessary here'.*[94] He noted, too, that her religious faith had deepened. He felt this shift towards a more religious viewpoint on life was something she needed and he wrote of his thoughts at the time a long time later:

> *She had lost her father in childhood; her mother's death and then her brother's left her all alone; she lacked help and consolation.*[95]

She returned to Dundee with a renewed strength, uplifted sense of spirit, and an odd-looking grey and black uniform, which she had worn with the Grey Ladies, where D'Arcy had so admired it, and which would be her almost constant state of dress until she died.

Almost as soon as she returned she attended the meeting of DSU that was held annually in May. It can well be imagined that the members who were present would be looking forward to the stories Mary Lily would have for them, and to welcoming her back to the fold. They would not have expected the address she delivered:

> we may be divided into workers and parasites, the former class comprising those who in any way add by their activity to the output of the manifold life ... and the latter, those who live on the labour, that is, the life of others. Amiable and cultured lives though they may be, they are the lives of parasites ... It is the merest truism to say that we women of leisure are living on the lives of others. The food we eat, the frocks we wear, are literally so much of the life of others – for ten hours a day, week in, week out, is the bigger part of life ... Work is the only end of all culture, all sensibility ... And at this present time the outlet which is the nearest, and which presents the strongest claim is undoubtedly social work.

This delivery was aimed at those in the Union and those present that evening, but it was undeniably a naked attack on the parasites of Dundee's wealthy elite too; those who enjoyed *'cultured lives'* at the expense of those who toiled hard, ten hours a day, week in, week out. The nearest thing to living the life of the worker, working those long poorly paid hours, was fighting their corner through social work.

This was a far more vehement piece of rhetoric than anything Lily had spoken before, though the response from further afield than the Social Union membership is unregistered. Whether or not this made any difference to the attitudes of the *'parasites'*, it certainly engendered a great deal more energy from the ranks of the membership and helped to attract new members. Public lectures, with prominent guest speakers, were organised, and apparently had the desired effect of raising awareness of the DSU's ethos. By 1905 the membership had risen to 168, which was over a hundred more than had been the case seven years earlier. By the following year it was 197 and it rose, by the year of Mary Lily Walker's death, to a peak of over 300 members, 120 of whom had volunteered to be house-visitors, or helpers, or rent collectors.

Mary Lily was firmly in the driving seat at the DSU by the mid-1900s, and she began to move the focus of its activities towards the plight of mother and child welfare. Her own energies appeared boundless and her ideas for change were beginning to shape themselves. Her most important decision around this time was to found a Grey Lodge Settlement House. This development would allow Lily to train and employ full-time social workers, meaning the Union would no longer be totally at risk from the vagaries of volunteer workers. To enable this, she bought a large stone-built villa in Dundee's Wellington Street, a street which ran down to Victoria Road, one of the main arteries of Dundee, commonly used for the transportation of raw jute to the factories and mills which proliferated at the top of this road, and into its continuation which became Dens Road. Names like Eagle Jute Mill, and Rashiewell, Caldrum Works and Bowbridge; all were mills that relied on this street for the import and export of product.[96]

Once the house was bought, Lily uttered an ultimatum to the Union. She wanted them to finance the board and training for two students, while she would do the same for one. This would make a force of four, including herself, and she would be able to pass on the lessons learnt in social work in London. She urged the Union to accept, and offered the following words as final persuader: *'Without some such support and response I cannot continue'*. It was no great surprise when the DSU acceded to her demands.

Mary Lily furnished a little oratory in the house though she did not in any way try to get others to share her religious expression. She kept in contact with the Grey Ladies, and though it was not something she spoke of very much, she named the house after the settlement. Grey Lodge was the new name for the villa at 9 Wellington Street and it would be home to Mary Lily Walker for the rest of her life. Her ownership of Grey Lodge and her importance to the DSU gave her a position of power, and allowed her to demand that *'no work should be undertaken, no class started without my consultation and permission'*, but this had more to do with a desire to keep a focused approach within the Union than to express any dictatorial pressure. The purchase of Grey Lodge, and the training of social workers, gave a springboard for Lily to look to further ways of combating the poverty and dreadful living conditions of so many of Dundee's citizens and, to that end, she took on another challenge.

Of all her excellent achievements, there was one in particular which brought Mary Lily Walker to national attention. The initiative that had the greatest impact on the whole of the country was her 'Report on Housing & Industrial Conditions in Dundee', the compilation of which she shared with Miss Mona Wilson. This Report was commissioned by Dundee Social Union, although Lily helped to finance it and almost certainly persuaded the DSU to undertake it. It was overseen by its Social Enquiry Committee which was full of illustrious people from the fields of Education, Medicine, and from Social Reform.

The Enquiry which informed the Report was started in 1904 and completed in 1905. Mary Lily was the Honorary Superintendent of the Housing Dept of DSU, and Mona Wilson was designated as Superintendent of Enquiry. The task of writing up the various strands of information fell squarely on their shoulders. Mona, at 32 years of age, was nine years younger than Mary Lily when the project began, and while there were some remarkable similarities in the lives and backgrounds of the two women, there were also areas of great difference. They were brought together in this Report, and though they worked many hard hours, reporting on the most distressing of things, the relationship between them seems to have always been very cordial. Mary Lily was to remember Mona in her will, bequeathing her an upright desk from the drawing room of Grey Lodge, a picture by Shannon which Mona had admired, and a special set of a teapot, stand, sugar basin and cream jug. These were all marked W.W. and may well have belonged to Mary Lily's grandfather, William Walker, signifying the enormous regard Mary and Mona had for each other. Mona Wilson, after the untimely death of Lily, remembered the difficulties and obstacles that they had jointly managed to overcome in the course of writing the Report, but she remembered even more clearly the lady that Mary Lily was:

> she was also, and it is a rare combination, one of the best persons in the world to play with … able to shop away with her Grey Ladies uniform and enjoy both the peace of her cottage at Gauldry and the travels abroad.[97]

Mona Wilson was born in Rugby, and was educated at Clifton School, before going to St Leonard's School in St Andrews. In 1892 she matriculated at Newnham College, Cambridge, where she remained until 1896, though she took no examinations while she was there. This was not an unusual situation at the time. Like Mary Lily, she had a father who married again after the death of his first wife, though Mona had stepbrothers whilst Lily had half-sisters. Whilst Mary Lily's father was a solicitor, Mona's father was a Headmaster, and he was also a clergyman of the Church of England, which of course had been the church of Mary Anne Allen before she married Thomas Walker.

The two women shared a passion for social work, Mona having taken part in an investigation of social conditions in West Ham, London, in 1902. Before that, Mona had joined the Women's Trade Union League as its secretary in 1899 where, under the auspices of the Industrial Law Committee, she compiled a handbook of the legal regulations affecting the working conditions of women employed in factories and other places. Her preface to this handbook stated that she

> intended to inform district visitors, deaconesses, mission workers, residents in settlements, helpers in friendly societies and working girls' clubs, and other social workers of what the legal rights of women workers were, so that they could alert the factory inspectorate when the regulations were not complied with.

The mention of *'residents in settlements'* particularly chimes with Mary Lily's work, but for Mary Lily it was the conditions of housing and the plight of women and children that were the main drivers.

One other area of particular difference between Mary Lily and Mona was in their outside interests. Apart from her interests in cycling and walking in the hills, Mary Lily steeped herself in the battle to bring about a betterment in the conditions of those she felt most needed it. There is no mention of her being particularly interested in the theatre or the arts, apart from one reported visit she made to a classical music concert.[98] Mona, on the other hand, boasted a great friendship with the well-known writer Thomas Sturge Moore (1870–1944) and through him made a series of acquaintances from his literary and artistic circle. Such was the attraction of this "other" part of her life, that Mona described her work in social investigation and administration as *'uncongenial'*.[99]

The physical toll on the two women writers of the Report was considerable, and Mona particularly found her time in Dundee to be both mentally and physically enervating. She had no one to share her love of literary works and events, and, for her, *'time passed so slowly'*. Her description of Dundee, and its conditions that she was charged to write on, reveal the pressures she felt herself under. She said that the town was *'the most depressing place you can possibly imagine'*, and though she hoped that her involvement would help to alleviate the social ills and deprivation she found in Dundee, deep down she felt that *'things here are altogether past praying for'*. Mona Wilson can hardly be blamed for having these thoughts, for while she shared Mary Lily's passionate desire for social reform, this was not her hometown, and these were not her fellow citizens. Whilst waiting for the proofs of the Report to be completed, the pair took off for Holland, where they were *'too tired to do anything but lie among the pansy plants during slow journeys on a barge'*.[100]

Mona took an *'enforced'* holiday in France as soon as the Report was concluded because she felt she had to *'do something cheerful before I settle down to a new job'*. She felt journalism was much easier to write and to read than the *'colourless'* facts that Social Reform had to report on. Mary Lily Walker, contrastingly, redoubled her efforts to work on behalf of the poor and helpless, and contrived to think up new initiatives in this quest.

Miss Mona Wilson was appointed to the National Insurance Commission in 1910. Her £1000 per annum salary, exactly the same as her male counterparts, made her the highest-paid woman civil servant of the time, and she was one of the first to receive equal pay. In 1917 she was seconded to the secretariat of the newly formed Ministry of Reconstruction. She went on to become the first woman assistant secretary at the Ministry of Reconstruction, and acted as secretary to various committees which had sprang up for co-ordinating the voluntary and professional sectors of women's social work during and just after the First World War. As one of the most senior women civil servants, she found that her views on policy issues affecting women carried some weight. She was always happy to concede that her difficult and daunting time in Dundee, and her work on the Social Report which she shared with Miss Mary Lily Walker, were very influential in the development of her career and her decisions of conscience.[101]

The Report looked at five specific areas of concern in Dundee in 1904–5. Firstly, Housing Conditions were examined and reported upon. The second line of examination was Family Income and Expenditure at the time. Thirdly, the issue of Employment and Wages was considered. The fourth line of enquiry was Women's Labour and Infant Mortality, and lastly, the findings obtained from a Medical Inspection of Schoolchildren were reported on. Within the final category, there were six particular considerations:

1. *A General Report by Mary L Walker and Mona Wilson*

2. *A Medical Report by Chas Templeman – Medical Officer of Health (Dundee)*

3. *Medical Examination of Boys – Alexander Low, M.B., C.M.*

4. *Medical Examination of Girls – Emily C Thomson M.B., C.M., L.R.C.P.S.*

5. *Report on Ears, Nose & Throat – G Taylor Guild, M.B., C.M.*

6. *Report on Eyes – E F McLeod Neave M.D. & W Foggie M.A., M.B., C.M.*

Mary Lily Walker, when she wrote of bad ventilation, insanitary closets, and filthy ash-pits in houses and tenements, based her conclusions on empirical evidence. When she mentioned the evils of overcrowding, the utmost lack of privacy, and a level of drunkenness that suggested Dundee had thirty percent more deaths from alcoholism than the average for Scotland, she had witnessed these with her own eyes.

The Report shows that half of the houses in Dundee in 1904 had two rooms. Dundee had 19,503 such houses, which was proportionately more than any of the other three major cities of Scotland. When it came to houses of four rooms or more, Dundee, with 4,352, had significantly less of these than the others. In Edinburgh, a third of houses had two or more rooms, but in Dundee it was scarcely one in ten. In Dundee's two-roomed houses dwelt 83,367 people – that equated to an average of 4.3 people per house.

There were 813 one-roomed houses in Dundee with more than five people living in them (there were three one-roomed houses found to have ten people dwelling in them). Over 300 two-roomed houses in Dundee had nine or more people living there. Overcrowding within houses was rife and Dundee was the worst of any city in Scotland. Half the people in Dundee were living more than two to a room. It should also be noted that some of these houses were not just the habitations of humans; the keeping and even the breeding of dogs in these cramped conditions was not unusual. Neither was the keeping of cats or pigeons, and there is the certainty of unwelcome mice and rats being abundantly present. All of these figures would spread surprise and alarm to those across the country who read them, but they would not have surprised the committee at Dundee Social Union in the least.

For the purposes of the enquiry, 5,888 houses in Dundee were selected for survey. The choice of areas in Dundee to be selected for the survey was left to Dr Templeman and Councillor Elliott (ex-Convenor of the Sanitary Committee). One was chosen in the west of the city, running south from Lochee Road to Perth Road, and west from the Overgate to the top of Hawkhill, whilst the other chosen area took in the area to the north of Seagate as far as Constitution Street, and east from Bell Street to Dens Road. Two Municipal Health visitors, qualified as Sanitary Inspectors, were combined with two ladies, both certificated by the Incorporated Sanitary Association of Scotland, as the group to carry out visits and to record evidence. Almost all the properties were blocks of flats or tenements, simply because that was, by far, the most common dwelling arrangement in Dundee.

Mary Lily's hand can be seen in the Report into housing conditions. There were four or five distinct types of buildings, and the suitability of these for housing was very diverse. In the worst of these, the tenants were generally unskilled and the population tended to shift house more regularly. The Prudential Assurance Society was kind in helping the DSU to discover the extent of some of the problems when they revealed '*blacklisted*' properties. The list of houses they would not insure lives included '*31 entire streets, or courts*' in Dundee, and there were also fifty-two streets where some blocks would not be covered because '*the death-rate, and especially the infant death-rate, is particularly high*'.[102] With the dreadful state of houses came the dreadful state of sanitation, and the Report included some harrowing facts.

Of all the 5,888 houses visited by the appointed ladies, not one had a bathroom. Many houses had no running water inside them, and whilst some had taps on the stairwell, many had to use standpipes in the communal yard. Even in the best of blocks, ash-pits where human waste was deposited were uncovered, leaving a stench that was reported to be '*overpowering*'. The Dundee Sanitary Inspector's Report of 1903 cited some of the examples to be found at the time. One property that housed 177 persons had no sanitary accommodation whatsoever. A property with 346 tenants had four privies between them. Another property, one that housed 215 people, had only one privy. In many of these houses the inhabitants kept a pail for waste. This would remain in the house all day until it would be delivered to the bottom of the block where scavengers would empty it every night. Having waste in a house all day has obvious health and social implications and the question of decency and modesty was also an issue. In a house where the rooms, including the kitchen, have sleeping accommodation, it is easy to imagine the levels of personal and moral degradation that arose.

The section of the Report which covered Family Income and Expenditure described a host of instances where hand-to-mouth living was the norm. This section looked at incomes and number of dependents in three categories: firstly, where there was one male wage earner in a family; secondly, where only one female wage earner was the supporter of a family; and lastly, families with two wage earners (husband and wife). The facts made disturbing reading, especially in the first and second categories. In the case of the male wage earner, 390 of 769 cases showed the earnings to be lower than £1 per week (112 of which had under 15 shillings), but in the case of a female wage earner, 655 of 684 cases had less than 15 shillings per week (197 had less than 10 shillings per week). In some eleven families, where the woman was the wage earner, more than five people in one household were trying to live off less than 10 shillings per week. Finding out and listing these figures must have been a distressing business. Rent and coal together ran to an average of around 5 shillings per week, so any family under the 10 shillings wage mark would have to feed and clothe everyone for less than 5 shillings per week. For a family exceeding five in number that seems incredible.

The Report used the 1901 census as a base for estimating population by employment and this threw up some remarkable information. The total number of people aged 10 and over in Dundee was 126,400. Of that, 53,677 were male, and there were 72,723 females in the city. This in itself made Dundee an unusual place. There were 9,000 more men in employment than women, and they outnumbered women in all occupations with two exceptions. Domestic Service was, predictably, an occupation where far more women traditionally worked, and in Dundee there were 3,007 women compared to 360 men at work. Textile Fabrics was the other occupation to feature more women than men, but the extent of the difference was hugely significant. Figures showed that of 84,000 people at work in all occupations in Dundee, almost 40,000 worked in textiles. In that figure of 40,000, only just over 12,000 were males. This figure for males is misleading in that many boys, even up to the end of teenage years, worked in this industry, but were allowed to leave as they grew into adulthood. The number of adult wage earners working in the factories and mills would have been close to three women for every man. With the Report showing that women generally earned much less than men it became all too obvious why owners of mills and factories perpetrated this imbalance, and why so many families were so far under the poverty line.

The sheer level of detail in the Report was a striking feature, and comparative wages by occupation, by gender and by age were listed for many of the forms of employment in the city. Also listed were average food and fuel prices, using two different supplier outlets, and typical rents for the town by property type. These two chapters, on Family Income and Expenditure, and on Employment and Wages, made interesting if depressing reading when considering the impact on a beleaguered community. The following chapter, on Infant Mortality, was no less so.

Dundee had more women in occupation per capita than any other city in Scotland. This equated to fifty-five percent of all women, and no other city came close (Paisley at forty-four percent was second). Dundee also held the dubious distinction of having the highest rate of illegitimate births at eight percent. Illegitimate children in Dundee showed a mortality rate of 354 per 1000, whilst the children of married couples died at the rate of 144 per 1000. In the cases of the illegitimate children who had died, six out of the sixty-two deaths were known to have occurred from smothering due to overlaying.[103] Seventeen had died of being immature at birth, three from syphilis contracted from mothers, and twenty-five had died of gastric conditions. Thirty-seven of the total were fed from birth on artificial milk. Other distressing figures showed that across 331 sampled families, the women had delivered 1,345 babies to date but 715 of these children had died, and only 85 of the 715 had reached their first birthday. The Report went on to look at schooling and the cleanliness of these places, and the effect that "half-time" working had on the health of children. Medical examinations were done on girls and on boys, which listed the sorts of illnesses and infections that affected the population of children in different locations in Dundee. Ears, noses and throats were tested, as were their eyes, and often the examinations were hampered by the fact that many children were sewn into their clothes because lost buttons were too expensive.

In the end, Dundee Social Union, through the work of its house visitors and its medical professionals, through the effort of its Social Enquiry Committee (which included D'Arcy Thompson, Stegall, and Agnes Husband), through its convenors, Alexander Mackay and Sir R H A Ogilvy, Bart., but most especially through the sterling work of Mona Wilson, *'Superintendent of Enquiry'*, and Mary L Walker, *'Honorary Superintendent of the Housing Department'*, produced a Report which would inform meetings in Parliament. It would be read by, and would impress, all the major social reformers in the United Kingdom, but would be received with opposition in the town of Dundee.

Some used it as a tool to blame *'lazy, ignorant'* working-class mothers for the woes of the city.[104] Others, including the newspapers, blamed the working-class man for the malaise, often in demeaning terms:

Undeterred by his gloomy prospects he marries, and becomes partially or solely dependent upon the wages earned by his wife. His future misery is the result of his own actions, and it would be reasonable to compel him to remain a bachelor until he is in receipt of a living wage for two or more persons as it would be to compel his wife's employer to make provision for the matrimonial inconveniences to which she is naturally subject.[105]

This article in the conservative-orientated *Courier* discounted the difficulty for men in getting jobs, and sympathised with the employer for women leaving to have babies.

Many in the city thought the DSU had overstepped the mark in issuing such a damning Report that was declared to be *'an opprobrium upon the city'* in the *Dundee Advertiser* of 30th March 1906. Mary Lily Walker responded to the criticism and the complaints by asking the simple question of her detractors: *'Are the Statements true?'* It was the empirical basis of Lily's work that gave her Report its uniqueness. Such detailed, systematic work impressed other social reformers, because it was written with the advantage of the scientific training that Lily had received in University College's classrooms and laboratories.

The town authorities and the School Board either procrastinated on improving the conditions highlighted in the report, or ignored them entirely.[106] It would be much further afield that the merit of the Report would find favour and gather respect. Ramsay MacDonald, who would be the future Labour Prime Minister, cited the Report in parliamentary speeches, as did *'others in that House'*.[107] What did impress commentators was the way Lily and Mona blamed conditions rather than people for the dismal situation. Alcohol and drunkenness was a serious problem in the town, as it had been for scores of years, but Lily turned the problem back on conditions when she wrote: *'We are repeatedly told that drink is at the root of these miserable homes, but in many cases it is the miserable conditions of life that send husband and wife to the public-house'.*[108]

In later years D'Arcy Thompson would evaluate Mary Lily's contribution to this remarkable Report:

There was no hiding the poverty in Dundee, but Lily Walker told the story word for word in the Report which she and Mona Wilson published in 1904 ... It gave chapter and verse; it reduced to figures the lives of the people; it told of unemployment and its vicissitudes, of wages and expenditure and of diet; of overcrowding, of the lack of sanitation and the consequences thereof ... The part dealing with housing and sanitation was uglier still. Of nearly 6000 houses inspected, over 550 (10 per cent) had no sanitary accommodation whatsoever, not even of the most primitive kind ... in another 15% there was rough (sanitary) accommodation for the men only ... There were some to whom these investigations were unwelcome, but no one questioned the plain facts which Miss Walker had set down.[109]

Possibly the most disturbing thing about the Report was that the areas chosen, the *'nearly 6000 houses'* spoken of by D'Arcy, were in Tay Street, Park Lane and Blackness Road, and these were not considered to be the worst areas of town. "The Overgate", an area mooted to hold *'the more flagrant evils of Dundee'*, was the subject of an Improvement Scheme, but sadly this did not start before the death of Mary Lily Walker.[110] Had "The Overgate" been included in the Report, findings may have stooped to greater depths.

જી ભ

Lily's achievements in promoting better conditions included many things that proved to be successful, and were taken on by other organisations. The Women's Hospital, which had grown from the tiny dispensary in the Hilltown area, moved to excellent premises in Elliott Road and eventually became subsumed in the leviathan of the National Health Service. The Restaurants for Nursing Mothers, the first of their kind in this country, became the model for other places, and after partly funding them for a while they were taken over by the local authority in Dundee. D'Arcy Thompson, in his 1938 Presidential Address to Grey Lodge Settlement Association, spoke of the creation of *'Infant Clinics'*, the *'School for Cripple Children'*, and also of her *'Milk Depots for Children'* (the "milkie school") in Carnegie Street.

He might have mentioned too the Children's Country Holiday Committee where Lily had teamed up with a philanthropic organisation called the Pearson's Holiday Fund to take disadvantaged children away for breaks. They supplied money and she helped to convert this into holidays away for people who had never seen beyond the boundaries of their town. Not all of her efforts succeeded; free school meals, offered by towns in other parts of the country, were never something that the School Board in Dundee could accede to. A great deal of effort and involvement of many people in reform failed to shift the Board away from their conviction that the feeding of school children was the responsibility of the parent. The Invalid School would go on to become Fairmuir Special School, and Dundee became the first in Scotland to have *'a fully organised municipal infant health service'* after Lily's initiatives were brought together.[111] Managing to keep all of these facilities together was testimony to Lily's breadth of thought, but there were still battles to be fought against the stubbornness and intransigence of many who held office in Dundee.

The only known photograph of Mary Lily Walker, shown here in the habit of Grey Ladies College, which she wore as her daily working uniform in the latter years of her life

Sunnybank, Mary Lily's childhood home on Magdalen Green, Dundee. She would have watched the Tay Rail Bridge being constructed from these windows

Dundee from the top of the Law, showing the jute mills and the original Tay Rail Bridge, completed in 1877, collapsed in 1879

Interior of a jute mill. The majority of jute mill workers were very low-paid women and children

Conditions were deplorable in the tenements of Dundee. Barefoot children were commonplace, with sometimes a single lavatory being shared by over 200 people

Dundee's strong economy made its shopping districts busy

Stewart's Court in 1876, looking from the Seagate towards Gellatly Street, depicting the demoralising conditions that drove so many of the population to drink

The local population turns out for a special occasion. Despite the wearing of "Sunday best" many children still go barefoot

In comparison to its deprivation, Dundee showed off its wealth when the Rt Hon W E Gladstone MP opened the Dundee Fine Art Exhibition in October 1890

Mary Lily Walker attendance at Dundee High School for two years and won academic prizes and acclaim for her abilities

The Whiteleys in Perth Road were the first buildings occupied by the newly-formed University College, Dundee

Prof D'Arcy Wentworth Thompson, Mary Lily's close friend and confidant throughout her adult life. D'Arcy was, at 24, the youngest of the Professors appointed to the new University College, Dundee

The professorial staff at University College in 1889. **Back row** *(l to r)*: John Steggall, Patrick Geddes, Alfred Ewing, Andrew Paterson and Percy Frankland. **Front row** *(l to r)*: D'Arcy Thompson, Principal William Peterson and Thomas Gilray. Five of the nine staff were members of the Dundee Social Union and thus personal friends or colleagues of Mary Lily Walker

Some the first year intake of students with Professor Steggall at University College, Dundee in 1883. A quarter of day students were women. Mary Lily may be amongst the students in this photo, as well as her older half-sister, Grace Walker, the oldest student to have matriculated, at the age of 49

Students in the chemistry laboratory at University College, Dundee during the early years of the College (*circa 1890*). It is possible that the young woman on the right is Mary Lily, who won three prizes in this subject

Members of the Maria Grey College for Women, Blackheath, London, in their traditional grey habits. Mary Lily Walker's time at the College (1898–1899) was crucial in developing a vision for her work in Dundee

The first Nursing Mothers Restaurant in Dundee, established by Mary Lily Walker as an attempt to increase women's opportunities to care for and breastfeed their newborn babies, thereby reducing infant mortality

The original Grey Lodge building in Wellington Street, bought by Mary Lily Walker in 1903 as a centre for training Dundee's first social workers

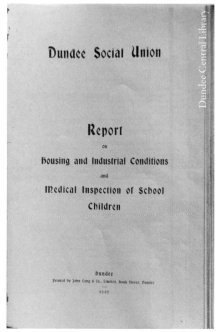

Dundee Social Union

Report
on
Housing and Industrial Conditions
and
Medical Inspection of School
Children

Dundee
Printed by John Long & Co., Limited, Bank Street, Dundee
1905

The frontispiece of the groundbreaking report written in 1905 by Mary Lily Walker and Mona Wilson. The report, commissioned by the Dundee Social Union, still remains the most requested item in the Local History Section of Dundee's Central Library

x

© DC Thompson & Co., Ltd.

Mourners leaving St Paul's Cathedral, having attended the funeral of Mary Lily Walker on 5 July 1913. She had worshipped at St Paul's throughout most of her life. This photograph apeared in the local *Advertiser*, which also featured tributes written by friends

'The Spirit of Mary Lily Walker' – Memorial Cross, Balgay cemetery, marking the burial site of Mary Lily Walker and three members of her family: her mother Mary Ann Allen, her brother Arthur and her half-sister Grace

© Brett Housego

First cohort of Social Workers at Grey Lodge Settlement 1916, illustrating the continuation of Mary Lily Walker's work following her death

Private collection, C. Spencer

Pictured by Mary Lily Walker's headstone in the Balgay Cemetery are the researchers who have brought this remarkable story to light: *(l to r)* Dr David Dobson, Pete Kinnear, Dr Suzanne Zeedyk and Eddie Small, the author

© Brett Housego

Chapter 5

In the Lions' Den

When Mary M Paterson first met Mary Lily Walker, the initial contact was one of awkwardness. At the time, Paterson thought this might be because she was one of HM Inspectors of Factories, and therefore from an industry-led environment, whilst she saw Mary Lily as a *'church-woman'* primarily because of the Grey Habit she wore. It soon became clear that the awkwardness was because Mary Lily was simply a very shy person and, according to Mary Paterson, this was something she never totally overcame in her life. This makes the story of Lily, and the achievements she managed, all the more remarkable. But, wrote Paterson, *'once the shyness was overcome, friendship was lasting and profound wherever Lily found it'*.

Lily's childhood days were spent in a household of older people. Her father, who had lived through times of strong Victorian values, would hardly have been likely to spend much time with his daughter, and besides, he was a busy businessman in a busy town. Her mother, complying with the customs of the day, would possibly have left much of her daughter's day-to-day needs to the nursemaid employed to look after her. Her sisters were old enough to be her mother. In fact Anna Louisa and Eliza, by the standard of the day, were both almost old enough to be her grandmother. This would have meant that a mutual sisterhood between them was unlikely to be felt until Lily was much, much older. Any natural shyness that she had would not be easily expunged in such a household. Her brother, Arthur, four years her junior, turned out to be, and probably always was, someone who found social interaction acutely difficult. Any love shown to him by his naturally caring sister seemed not to have been strongly reciprocated, and this must have given Lily sadness and distress at times. The Walker household was dominated by women by the time of Lily's tenth birthday: her brother was boarded at Glenalmond College in Perthshire, and her father was increasingly succumbing to dementia.

The first strong friendship that Mary Lily made outside the family home appears to have been with Meta Peterson. According to the census details, the Walkers, Mary Anne and her two children were living at 10 Airlie Terrace, Dundee in 1881, and the Petersons probably arrived to live nearby the following year. They came to Dundee from Edinburgh because Meta's brother had been appointed first Principal of the fledgling University College. Mary Lily and Meta were only separated in age by one year, but it is not recorded whether the friendship blossomed prior to their first days at university, or as a result of both being there. Meta's brother Magnus also enrolled that first year, and he had the honour and privilege of being student No. 1 in the first ever role of students, whilst his sister was No. 2. Meta knew Lily as well as anyone could at that time, and was to recall the early days of their friendship:

> When I first knew Mary Lily Walker ... she was, like most young women of our time, fully occupied with the duties that filled the life of daughter and sister. Her school education had been of the ordinary type, good as far as it went but not looking beyond the ties of home.[112]

These words paint a picture of a quiet and obedient girl, wholly taken up in, and accepting of, the typical role of a daughter in a middle-class family. The description of her education ties in with comments made by one of her university tutors, D'Arcy Wentworth Thompson, who described Lily as being *'of the simplest, homeliest upbringing'*. Her mother was an invalid, which would have meant that Lily's life was centred round her education and her mother's care.

Lily and her mother moved out of the family home at Sunnybank soon after half-sister Eliza married John Duff Bruce, leaving Grace to stay with the couple. Why they felt the need to move is unclear. It might simply have been to allow Eliza to be the mistress of her own home. It may even have had something to do with Mary Anne's infirmity. Whatever the reason, contact between Lily and her stepsisters would have been less frequent, which would make the opportunity to advance and develop her education at the new University College a welcome one. It is likely that Mary Lily's intelligence was recognised by her family, and that they would have encouraged her participation in further education. Interestingly, Grace matriculated along with Mary Lily and their brother for the first ever year of the College. Grace was, by some years, the oldest woman to enrol in that first year, and it is quite likely that her decision to do so was to support and encourage the shy Lily. Her appetite for education was boundless and the choice of subjects she undertook demonstrated that she wanted to know as much as she could. The atmosphere in those first few weeks and months in this brand new educational establishment must have been charged with excitement.

It probably helped Mary Lily that all the students were new to University College. Her shyness may have gone unnoticed in this coming together of strangers, but it is noticeable in the many black and white photographs which memorialise those early times that Mary Lily Walker's name is unmentioned in any key to these pictures. She was not keen to be photographed it would seem. It also helped her that almost all of the lecturers and tutors were young; her awe for their erudition would not be added to by any sense of awe for their advanced years spent in academic life. Making friends would not be hard when everyone was imbued with trepidation and anticipation, and the cohort of women students must have felt a strong sense of bonding in the unique experience of the classrooms. They would know that theirs was the first University in Scotland to allow both sexes to share classrooms, and this sense of pioneering would heighten the whole experience. The sense of liberation would have been exhilarating. Barriers were being broken, and neither custom nor social mores could undo this. A few years earlier and this would have been unthinkable, but if this gender realignment could be achieved, then many more things might also be.

Meta Peterson remembered Lily having her *'intellect quickened'* by the spur of academic life. Lily's life was filled with two things in these early days: the thirst for knowledge and looking after her invalid mother. She studied Latin and Mathematics initially, then after a year she moved to Biology and Chemistry. Her prize-winning exploits indicate that she was conscientious and intellectually bright, and her eclectic choice of courses show she desired to learn all she could. But Meta always felt that Lily's *'interests'* at University were always *'subsidiary, for she was in the first place the devoted daughter'.*[113] Her study widened into Embryology and Botany and her classes meant contact with several of the professors. D'Arcy Wentworth Thompson described her as *'an excellent student; she learned a great deal of Natural History; I have only had three or four students as good ... in all my years of teaching'.* This was high praise indeed, as it was written by Thompson in 1938, approaching fifty years after he had taught Mary Lily, and the number of students he had taught during his long career must have been very high.[114] Further evidence of her success at university came in papers and articles which she had published. In one publication in particular, Lily wrote a piece entitled 'On the Form of the Quadrate Bone in Birds' and in a second article for the same book she wrote 'On the Larynx of the Monotremata'.[115] The quality of her work brought the praise from Thompson that he would have altered nothing, nor could he have improved it.

Whether Mary Lily gave much thought to the future, and to the days after her university days were finished, seems unlikely. Devotion to her mother would have prevented such thoughts, and she came from a family where women did charitable works rather than paid employment. There would have been no reason to think beyond her immediate interests until her mother passed away. This was a very distinct milestone in Lily's life. She had already begun to get involved with the newly formed Dundee Social Union through her association with Professors Thompson, Carnelley and Stegall. There can be no doubt that the sort of things they planned to do, and the cause they were doing it for, was something she'd found both rewarding and fulfilling. Meta Peterson thought that Mary Lily's loss of her mother presented her with a choice of utilising her exceptional ability to gain academic distinction, or venturing into social service. In Meta's words, it became *'a question between living for self and living for others'*. Mary Lily Walker decided her future lay in living for others.[116/117]

Lily gave up on a B.Sc. degree at St Andrews, despite the fact that it was almost completed and that she had been doing as well as she always did. This was almost certainly a decision that was made because her mother had passed away, rather than any rush to get into DSU work, and for the year after her loss she travelled and stayed away from Dundee for quite a lot of the time. It is likely that James Allen, her mother's brother, came to Dundee for the funeral along with other aunts and uncles, as the service was held three days after her death, a day later than was normal at the time.[118] It is also very likely that he would have stayed in Dundee a few days after the service, and that Mary Lily would have accompanied him back. Letters from D'Arcy Thompson to Mary during the year of 1889 (and there were very many of them) serve to plot her whereabouts during a year that must have been spent in some grief, and much meditation.

After an extended spell at her uncle's home, Bank Top, Lily spent three months staying at the Grange Hotel, in Grange-over-Sands, Lancashire. This was described as *'a delightful and fashionable Hotel in the Italian style of architecture ... having 70 rooms, also large refreshment rooms, stables, etc., swimming and other baths are fitted up and supplied with sea water'* in the 1876 Travel Directory. It was situated in a small town that had once been very difficult to access, but which had been transformed by the rail network. Lily seems to have been alone in this hotel; certainly she mentions no one else staying there with her in letters to D'Arcy. She did use some of her time there making drawings of "plates" to be used in D'Arcy's publications. After three months in the splendour of the Grange, she took a trip to London to stay with the Hildesheim family, where she was no doubt made very welcome. Olga and Evelyn, the daughters of this family, would eventually be left a bequest in Mary Lily's will.

After London, Mary Lily travelled back to Dundee to a house at 17 Airlie Place rather than the one at 9 Windsor Terrace that she had shared with her mother, and where Mary Anne Walker had died. The three months from July to September were spent between Dundee and Edinburgh. Some of the time in Dundee would be spent in visiting Sunnybank where her two sisters were still living alongside Eliza's husband, John Duff Bruce, and John's nephew, 17-year-old Robert Bruce. Eliza was still very active in charitable work where she sat on one or two Ladies' committees, particularly the Industrial School where she had long been featured. Grace, too, was very busily engaged in good works, and she was often to be found helping at YWCA functions.[119] Lily travelled to England twice more in the year of 1889; firstly to visit friends in Leamington, before going to Bournemouth in November to stay at the Marmion Hotel. The Marmion had not the splendour of the Grange though it was a reputable place. It was last mentioned in the 1934 Bournemouth Guide, and closed some two years later. From Bournemouth's sea air, bracing as it might have been in November, Lily went back to the Allens at Kendal, possibly to discuss Christmas plans. She then returned to Dundee in December before returning to Uncle James at Bank Top for her first Christmas without her mother.[120]

Mary Lily journeyed more in 1889 than she had ever done before, alternating stays with family and friends with stays on her own in seaside hotels. In thinking through her situation, she must have resolved to take up the challenge of work with the DSU rather than returning to more further education. She also moved home, this time to No 1 Windsor Street in Dundee. Windsor Street ran from Perth Road to Magdalen Yard Road, so was within easy reach of her two sisters in Sunnybank, but it was also very close to Anna Louisa who, by this time, lived with a domestic servant and a cook cum servant at No 8. Anna Louisa's welfare was a constant concern for Thomas, her father, something that was highlighted in the division of his estate after his death. Mary Lily, in moving to a house so near to Anna, was exhibiting the same caring attitude as her father. Anna Louisa had been the subject of a handbag theft in Dundee in 1888 which had attracted the lurid headline in the *Courier*: '*DARING STREET ROBBERS IN DUNDEE: SNATCHING LADIES' HANDBAGS*'.

On 24th May of that year two men, William Johnston and Patrick Hughes, had snatched the bag of Anna Louisa Walker in Dundee's Barrack Street. Apparently they had watched her emerge from a bank and go into shops in Bank Street. In snatching the bag, they got away with 10 pounds, 12 shillings and sixpence in cash, along with the bankbook, a silk scarf and a handkerchief. They were eventually apprehended some time later but the bag and contents were not recovered. Whilst this sort of incident would be distressing for anyone, it can only be imagined how stressful it must have been for the victim who had been mentally ill all her life, and, in turn, for her sisters.[121]

Anna Louisa's name would appear in a newspaper article once more in her lifetime when details of her estate were printed on the 1st November 1892. She had died, on February 27th 1892, after a battle with cancer which she'd suffered from for *'above two years'*. She passed away not at home but at Sunnybank, 61 Magdalen Yard Road, the house to which her father had moved his family almost thirty years earlier, and where Eliza and Grace lived. Her brother in law, John Duff Bruce, registered the death. Anna Louisa Walker had lived to be 70 years of age and was the first child of Thomas and his first wife Catherine. She would have been part of the Glasite congregation in Dundee, and would almost certainly have been baptized in the font in the chapel in King Street. Like her sisters Grace and Eliza, she latterly attended St Peters Church, and in her estate she left £1000 to the Treasurer of the Free Church of Scotland for their sustentation fund. This payment was *'subject to life-rent'* of her brother Arthur. He was forty-five years younger than Anna, but his assent was needed to guarantee the will of his oldest sister. Whilst many things were changing, the place of women in society was still as it had always been. Anna Louisa also left money (£1000) to Gartnavel Asylum, and separately gave £400 to the *'indigenous gentlewomen'* who were *'incarcerated there'*.

Arthur was not at Anna Louisa's funeral. Her half-brother was on a ship headed for New Zealand at the time, and he would therefore not have seen Anna's coffin being lowered into the ground at Western Cemetery where their father had also been interred. She left an estate valued at almost £6000, which, given that she had lived on private means, and kept a servant and sometimes two, suggests that Thomas Walker must have left all his family very well off. The death certificate for Anna Louisa was made out by J M Miller, M.D., who may well have attended to her quite regularly during her illness. In his time, Dr Miller also certified the deaths of her father, Thomas, and his wife, Mary Anne, and so he knew the family well. Mary Lily presumably knew about her oldest sister's cancer which would have been diagnosed just before Lily moved to be in the same street as Anna Louisa.[122]

After her year of *'visiting her friends and her mother's family'*, and her months of collecting her thoughts, Lily *'gave herself'* to the Dundee Social Union and became very enthusiastically involved in their work. She switched her tenacity and zeal to the tasks in hand through her role in the Housing Department which the DSU had formed. She became, wrote Meta Paterson, *'a sympathetic and generally welcome visitor and rent-collector'*. Just what she thought, and what she saw, on these first house visits is difficult to imagine, but whatever she experienced in those first few houses it was enough to make Mary Lily Walker devote her *'life and her powers'* to social reform and to the cause of Dundee women and their children. At this point Lily began to introduce other elements into her social work, including starting up clubs for mill-working girls.[123] She grew to realise that enthusiasm and amateur effort were not enough to tackle the enormity of the task which DSU had set itself. It would have been an easy decision to immerse herself in the immediacy of rent-collecting and sympathetic befriending amongst the properties they owned and managed. This would have been real social work, and anyone who wished to convince themselves that they were actively giving themselves to the poor and the destitute may well have stopped at that, but Mary Lily saw that a more professional attitude and better methods would yield greater benefits in the fight against the deplorable living and housing conditions so endemic in her hometown.

She must also have realised that the band of professors and academics who had started this extremely worthwhile concept were all hard-working professionals, and busy in their disparate fields of academia. Whilst these men were giving ideas and energy to the project, it could only be to the extent that other duties allowed. Lily could give more time than they might, and she could throw herself into it more than others could. She realised that her enthusiasm and energy alone would not bring sufficient progress, and that the visits around the doors of these Dundee tenements and the sights inside proved how desperately urgent was her task. The choice was simple enough; she would have to go to other places where this sort of work was being undertaken. D'Arcy Thompson would have made her aware of the settlement work in London that he had been connected with. The problem was that Mary Lily Walker was a very shy person, and it was only once she had become familiar with people and surroundings that she felt comfortable and able to effect changes. If she was going to go to London, then it would challenge her own introverted nature. It was a decision which would have been extremely difficult for her, and yet all too simple at the same time.

She went to the Women's University Settlement at Southwark in London, where she worked directly under the very able and highly respected Octavia Hill. She learnt a great deal that would make her a much more wise and effective organiser when she returned to the fray in Dundee. She went to Southwark in 1893 and spent many months under the woman who would offer her a wardenship of a settlement because she was impressed by Lily's intelligence and aptitude. Octavia Hill was different from Lily in very many ways (particularly in manner, where some would claim her to be demanding and autocratic) but the results she had produced in London were positive proof of the efficacy of her methods.[124] When she did return to Dundee, and to the desolation found in its tenements and in the inhabitants of these unfit properties, she began to put her own particular style of management and much more professional and organised approach to better effect. This meant adapting the practices she found in London to fit the milieu of Dundee. London's worst slums were equivalent to Dundee's, but Dundee had proportionately many more of these. This was less of a problem than the employment situation, as Dundee had a peculiarly high proportion of woman and half-time children in work. Mary Lily's thoughts on the matter were reported in the Ninth Annual Report of the DSU in 1896 where she wrote:

[In Dundee] *the mothers who should be in their homes taking care of their children, are all busy at the loom. No outsider can know all this horrible system means; we know a little but we are helpless, and wait.*

Lily felt that anyone who did not have to permanently live in these conditions could not possibly imagine the full horror of it. Anyone who did not have to work, as a matter, quite literally, of life and death, in the cacophonous noise, choking "stoor" and pathetically lowly-paid drudgery of the jute mills, couldn't ever hope to understand what they were truly like. Knowing she could sympathise but not fully understand the profoundness of their plight was painful, and knowing how much of the burden was placed on the mothers in this situation was more painful still.

The problems that had encountered rent-collectors and visitors in the early days of the DSU remained as problems in the 1890s. Findings which were reported to the Police Commission, who at this juncture were responsible under the

Dundee Police and Improvement Consolidation Act of 1882 for overseeing lighting and sanitation provision in the town, apparently made little difference. Stair lighting was often non-existent, and the lack of whitewashing meant that stairways were constantly dark, dingy places. This hardly encouraged tenants to perform their weekly washing of stairs, and many needed no encouragement to forget to take their turn. Whilst water provision into houses was improving, there were many areas in Dundee that awaited the service. However, the provision of standpipes had improved the quality of water. The area that still caused consternation was the lack of provision of even the most rudimentary toilet facility.[125] The battle to combat this situation was still in its infancy, and though Mary Lily had brought new and improved methods of tackling property and rent-collection management, there were times when, in the quiet of her evenings, she must have felt deflated.

Mary Lily's sojourn at Southwark had gained her several friends, and, as was her way, many of these became lifelong correspondents. Her time there had given her ideas, and a sense of belonging to a national movement; it brought her in touch with luminaries such as Charles Booth and Seebowm Rowntree, as well as Octavia Hill. But the task in hand grew in dimension as the number of voluntary members of the DSU and willing rent-collectors steadily diminished. More was needed, or at least some new impetus was needed, and when it came, it started with a tragedy.

A letter from Mary Lily to D'Arcy Thompson, dated August 17th 1897, reported on the death of Mrs Madge Valentine which had happened four days earlier.[126]

> *D'Arcy*
>
> *This is the very saddest letter in all our friendship ... and I hardly know how to do it. Oh if you had not been so*

terribly far away. Last week ... the fever rose again – and after battling for seventeen days Madge, who is for me the incarnation of life & hope & brightness died last Thursday.

It is tragic beyond words – I entered the house just as Mr Valentine [Madge's husband] came down stairs – the nurse brought poor Denny out & put her into my arms.

Since that evening I have felt nothing – realised nothing – Poor man – poor little Denny & oh the beautiful babies ... everything that makes it more bitter was there – the dread of infection – the unconsciousness – no message of farewell – the isolation – the protracted suffering. One cannot bear to think of it ... your friendship has brought many pleasant memories, but none I value like this. My friendship with Madge is one of the most perfect memory – there is no flaw, no jar from first to last – I loved her intensely & I hear from them all that she loved me too. I cannot write any more – my heart is just love for them all – come back quickly

Yours affectionately
M L Walker

This news was devastating for Mary Lily. Madge was Margaret Oliphant Valentine, wife of a partner in a jute manufacturing company in Dundee, and niece to Margaret Oliphant, a celebrated nineteenth-century writer and author. Denny was Madge's younger sister, though her full name was Janet Mary Oliphant. Madge's marriage to William Roderick Harris Valentine had produced three children: Margaret, known to the family as Princess (born 1894), William, known as Bob (born 1895) and Francis Cyril, less than three weeks old when his mother died of scarlet fever. This was a tragedy foretold in another letter from Mary Lily to D'Arcy, sent two weeks earlier on Wednesday 4th August 1897.[127]

Dear D'Arcy

We are in terrible trouble ... Madge is lying terribly ill – scarlet fever – it began when the baby was 2 days old – nobody know how that is a week ago & she is still fighting for life.

I met Dr Sinclair who was much cut up ... it is malignant and there is just a chance. For this to come after baby's birth was safe and well is too awful. For him, Mr Valentine – ~& Denny – it is heart-breaking ... Poor Princess and Bob are banished to a cottage – I have come along to sleep at Sunnybank in the absence of the family , so as not to infect the Hospital [Lily was staying in the Women's Hospital in Seafield Road at the time] *– I fear that everybody will think me a terrible fool for going near the house, but I love her dearly & if one can help them at all surely one may be forgiven for running the risk. Poor little Denny is more of a spectre than ever – I cannot see how she can hold out much longer.*

Goodnight dear friend ...

Yours ever
MLW

The content of the letters reveal just how close Mary Lily and D'Arcy were, and how she also valued her love for Madge so highly. The death of poor Madge from scarlet fever, later thought perhaps to have been contracted from a visiting nurse, was terrible enough, but coming so soon after the safe birth of her third child, the oldest of whom was only 3, made the loss and grief so much the harder to endure and to explain. The fear, too, of carrying the contagion of disease is something that must have been dreaded in Dundee. A third letter, earlier still, from Lily to D'Arcy brought news of a death in the same family, though one that was more expected and natural. The letter was dated 2nd July of the same year.[128]

Dear D'Arcy

The thing we feared was too true. Mrs Oliphant passed away on the 27th June ... a fortnight before the end the doctors acknowledged it was malignant – it was a great mercy that she was spared much & prolonged suffering – at the last she was free from pain & quite herself – cheerful & brave to the very end ... Mr Valentine ... wrote me that Madge & Denny were keeping wonderfully ... The papers all paid great tribute to nearly fifty years of literary work (Mrs Oliphant's) & so varied. Her personality impressed me more than the books & I'm glad it was that I was let in on the privilege and favour – else she was rather awe-inspiring.

I wonder what will happen to Denny – they will be glad enough to have her in Dundee & one room in the new part has always been appropriated to her. Madge will regret that Princess will not remember her grannie ... I am sure that it must have been a great relief to the old lady to know that there was a good honest man like Mr Valentine to look after both of them. Whatever he may lack in smooth seas I am sure he would be a great standby in such trouble.

The next letter, I trust, will be good news
Now goodbye – I feel it is a sad letter

Your affectionate friend
MLW

Mrs Oliphant had died at the age of 69 of cancer. She was prolific as a writer right up to her death, and her latest book was being proofed when she died. She was archetypically a Victorian matriarch who believed entirely in "breeding". She was aghast when her brother's daughter Madge (she had been mothering Madge and Denny since the death of their mother in 1870 when Madge was 7 and Denny only 5) decided to marry below her station. Although he was a partner in a lucrative company, and consequently very well off, Mrs Oliphant referred to him as *'The Tradesman'*. Madge had been 30 when she married Valentine, *'a man she did not love and who was not familiar with the artistic milieu in which she had been raised'* according to her aunt. Valentine's manner, his type of work, and his bourgeois establishment background offended her Victorian prejudices and ideas of breeding, and it grieved her that Madge had given up her *'long and expensive training as an engraver'* to marry him. In a quiet moment, however, Mrs Oliphant admitted to a friend that *'having one of the children married was an answer to a prayer, even if the bridegroom was not'*.[129] The sisters had been financially dependent on their aunt since 1870, and were orphaned in 1875 when their father died. Denny and Madge were both the objects of her aunt's love and affection; so much so that Denny changed her name by deed poll from Wilson to Oliphant, and often referred to her aunt as *'Dear Mother'*, as indeed did her sister.[130]

Mary Lily probably got to know Madge and Denny through Valentine, though the contents of letters might indicate that there was an introduction through D'Arcy. Valentine was from a prominent family in Dundee; one which branched into several areas of business. Mrs Oliphant had thought that Madge would suffer due to the "sort" of social and cultural comings together that Dundee was reputed to have. It was entirely possibly that Lily and Madge met at one of these tea-parties or social events.

The death of Madge, and the tragic circumstance of her loss, gave Mary Lily some sleepless nights and brought her to a decision that she announced to D'Arcy in one of their regular letters.[131]

4 Tay Square   April 12th [1897]

Dear D'Arcy

I am writing this because I would rather you heard my own way of it than gossip. – I have always wanted to get a year's training in nursing, but partly for my Uncle & partly for Meta have never seen a chance ... I think I shall just take it now – only I won't be all the time away from Dundee. – They will take me for some time at the 'New' in London, as we know some of the staff (women) there & there as the nurse at our little place will probably be one of our friends. I could finish there – I have always felt I should like to be able to look after the people one cares for when they need it, & it is always useful. Had Dr Raw not been such a stickler. I would have gone there – the wretch – and now I am going to say Something more which I want you to put away & forget for the present. & only remember when the time comes if it ever does which is not likely.

I can say it now because the world is going well with me & there are many friends & interests. But remember if ever you need one in trouble sickness or any other adversity, remember dear friend, that on my side there is the tie of a very deep affection, and nothing could be more than that you wanted one's help in any way & let outward things prevent.

I know this is a queer thing to write, but honestly it seemed like a burden hanging on me, & sometimes one should obey impulses. – Besides you know it well enough already, & its just as it was always – woe betide you if you ever allude to it.

However when you are very ill indeed you may be prepared to see me properly got up with mustard & a big bottle! – I think you will keep well ever after that threat.

After all one – very super-silious

Yours ever
M.L.W.

This letter was the nearest thing to a love letter that is still accessible in the collected letters of the pair. It was written from 4 Tay Square, which had once been the surgery of Dr Monro who had attended Francis Walker back in 1858, but had become the practice address of Doctors Emily Thomson and Alice Moorhead, the two medical officers at the Women's Hospital in Seafield Road. The loss of Madge seemed to have made Lily think of her lot, and of her relationships. The mention of Meta and of Uncle James seemed to symbolise the anchors that stopped Lily from letting her constraints go. Dr Raw was the Medical Superintendent at Dundee Royal Infirmary who had turned down an application from Lily to work in Dundee. The option of moving to London seemed to indicate that she felt the need for change. In offering herself to assist D'Arcy in *'sickness'* or in adversity, she is almost mimicking the lines *'in sickness and in health'* and she takes great pains in the letter to say that she is telling him something very special; *'something to remember when the time comes if it ever does'.*

She resigned from the Dundee Social Union, but it was not to go to work in a hospital. Instead she chose to move to the Grey Ladies Settlement in Blackheath, London. A letter from the Rev James Gilliand Simpson, Rector of St Pauls Episcopal Church in Dundee, the church where Mary Lily attended with her mother, explains the situation.[132]

7 Airlie Place, Dundee June 6, 1898

My dear Miss Walker,

I was glad to get your letter and to know that you had had a good holiday and were now settled to work in London. I agree with Miss Yeatman that your ultimate call seems to be to Dundee, and I had always looked forward to your return as a hope for the future.

But, as you know, it appeared to me that for more than one reason it was good for you to go away for a while before appearing in your new character as a regular church worker.

First a break with the past is good: you will come back to a certain extent as a different person. Secondly, something like a discipline and training is essential, if the enthusiasm of the amateur is to be tempered with the wisdom of the professional worker.

Thirdly, you are brought into touch with a larger church life by your connection with such an institution as Greyladies.

I am very anxious to see work covered on in lines of that kind here. I doubt whether sisterhood work, at least if carried on upon the All Saints' Method, is likely to be a permanent success.

But why not this other? There must be many like yourself who have no domestic ties yet who do not feel the call to a sister's life and vows. Why should not women work together in one congregation? What we require is women's work as regular and systematic as that of the clergy.

This response to a letter from Lily, a letter that is no longer in existence, reveals that she had found a stronger link to religion, although not one that would lead her to becoming a nun or even involved directly in church affairs. It seems that she was contemplating her future and considering the option of staying in London, or at least staying in the religious framework offered by the Grey Ladies movement. Miss Yeatman, to whom Simpson refers, was the warden in charge of the Grey Ladies College, which was situated at the time in Dartmouth House, formerly the residence of Lord Dartmouth before becoming the Palace of the first Bishop of Southwark. This building was in Dartmouth Road, immediately off Blackheath Hill, and the address was generally given as Blackheath Hill, or simply Blackheath.[133]

Miss Yeatman presumably suggested to Lily that a return to Dundee to carry out the same sort of work in her hometown might be the best option, and Rev Simpson's letter shows that he agreed. With the words of Yeatman and Simpson in mind, Mary Lily Walker returned to her hometown, imbued with new energy, strengthened by a personal renewal of faith, and with an appetite for a new challenge. Meta Peterson looked back at this time with the following memories:

> *When she returned to Dundee it was with the intention of making her home a branch of the Greyladies, a religious house working in connection with the Scottish Episcopal Church. Conditions were, however, less favourable than in London, and so workers were welcomed from other sources. This no doubt widened the sphere of service and usefulness.*[134]

Mary Lily's stay in London was not constant, and she came back to Dundee on a few occasions. On one such weekend at home she penned a letter to D'Arcy which revealed something of her mood, and it also showed how she was quite prepared to offer him mild rebukes when she felt he needed it.[135]

> *Sunnybank   7th Sept [1898]*
>
> *Dear D'Arcy,*
>
> *Why this 'thrauness' & what had happened to you – Do know you have not vouchsafed me a line all these five weeks – The least I can imagine is that you have injured your leg so much that you can't hold a pen! – as the immortal Spiers hath it.*
>
> *Now do write me whenever you get this or I shall really be quite angry. Now I have not much news.*
>
> *Dr Mackinnes the old man is to be married for the third time to the amazement of the Ferry.*
>
> *I was staying at Elmwood the babies were fascinating & poor Denny had her first spill with the bicycle – I suppose it is necessary to qualify – Now you have got something to do at*

the annual meeting of the Hospital but Denny will instruct
you when you return – I expect it will be to say a few nice
things about the doctors – but you will hear later on.

I was at the Steggalls last night he was distinctly wormwoodish
– Poor old Martin is still very ill –

I shall be up at Greyladies on the 14th – Blackheath Hill
S.E. Now I am just writing in a great hurry so farewell

Yours ever
M.L.W.

Five weeks without sending a letter was very unusual for
D'Arcy, and Lily made it plain that she took such a delay as
something to get angry about, although this was no doubt
written in a tongue-in-cheek way. This was an example of the
sense of humour which did not come into her relationships
with others until she felt comfortable. This was a very different
Lily from the one who left Dundee in a grief-stricken haste.
Her mention of Denny and the babies, and the fact she had
stayed some time at Elmwood, the home that Madge and her
husband stayed in and that Denny was still residing at, revealed
that she was glad to keep associations going. Her mention of
Professor Stegall, too, is interesting and indicates that friends
and colleagues, from no matter how far back, were never far
from her mind. Lily would not be at the annual meeting of the
Women's Hospital in 1898 because she would be in London
again with the Grey Ladies, continuing her aspirations to *'be
tempered with the wisdom of the professional worker'.*

Looking back on this period of the DSU and of the beginning
of the Grey Lodge era in Dundee, D'Arcy Thompson
commented on Lily's time in London. He had visited her
there and thought the grey habit she wore to be *'becoming'.*
This practice of wearing a habit may have given Lily a feeling of
security; something she could feel comfort inside. He saw that

she had deepened her religious faith in the *'Grey Ladies House'*, and he felt the void in her life after the death of her mother, and the painful loss of a very dear friend in Madge, was eased by her time away. He recalled that, though she seldom spoke of the Grey Ladies, despite having visits from several of those who had worked with her there, she named her house Grey Lodge in memory of those days.[136]

A letter from Greyladies at Blackheath, to D'Arcy, which was dated 27th November, gave Lily the chance to tell him about a new friend in her life:[137]

Greyladies   *Nov 27th [1898]*

Dear D'Arcy

I am having a quiet lazy Sunday as I have a cold so now write you a few lines. I liked your letter better than any gossip – though it made me feel very sad – for I didn't feel a bit to justifying the trust you put in me or the affection Denny gives so generously – I do not see clearly, or come to well-weighed conclusions alas! I only see very dimly & struggle & feel & struggle again to attain & translate into life the ideal of love & the fuller life that we all strive after. – It is not for everyone the quest of our lives – only I often regret that owing to circumstance & one's headstrong nature it is not just the natural & normal what it should be as you rightly said . – You see I feel one did not belong.

I would just gradually lose my touch here as one got more & more abandoned in Dundee. Besides as a rest to one's conscience & defence against absorbing things it is something to have ever that single rule of a day of! & one hot meal a day! – which are the most binding in the establishment!

Such a charming girl has come – a Miss Bethel – her brother was or is Governor of New Zealand – she is very beautiful, very thoughtful & much alive, paints & has seen much of varied life Before New Zealand – Switzerland – She is a great addition. –

Now goodnight as it is supper-time. I hope very much to be le même chose but better –

Your affectionate friend
M.L.W.

This missive heralded the arrival of Rhoda Bethell, the sister of the famed New Zealand writer, Ursula. Rhoda would later work in Dundee with Lily, and often share the hospitality of Gauldry weekends. To Lily, her family circumstances and her *'headstrong nature'* conspired to make her feel it was difficult to belong. By staying in London she would never belong, and it seemed that she felt she needed Dundee every bit as much as it needed her.

In May 1899, Mary Lily returned to Dundee. Her work in the capital had changed her life, and she was steeled to let her experiences benefit the DSU as well. She taught girls at St Paul's Episcopal School, and helped to tutor young women who were studying for B.Sc degrees at St Andrews University. These were things she would have found difficult prior to her time away, but she was resolved to make things work.[138] After 1900, letters from Lily to D'Arcy became shorter and more matter of fact, and they were filled with matters of business at the DSU or the Women's Hospital. In Myra Baillie's thesis,[139] she argues that this came about because of Lily's involvement at the Grey Ladies. Certainly there was a distinct cooling of their relationship when Lily went, and he wrote: *'You and I both know that you are clinging to the old beliefs to which all love and sorrow cling'*. Her decision, it seemed to him, was based on the need to fill an emotional void with spiritual succour. Either way, it also came at a time when D'Arcy was courting, and hoping to marry, Maureen Drury from Galway.[140]

119

Her first full year back in charge saw a revival in the number of members of the DSU, and a resilient determination from Lily. It also saw her introducing a series of lectures that did their job in reviving interest in the Union and its work. John Sinclair, MP for Forfarshire, was one speaker, and May Tennant, first woman factory inspector in England and wife of the Liberal MP and future Secretary of State for Scotland, H J Tennant, was another. Bringing this calibre of lecture-giver gave the DSU a sense of gravitas. It showed there was interest in its ideals and progress outside the town, and gave Lily the confidence to speak to people in, or connected to, public office.[141] The number of volunteers entering into the DSU increased exponentially; the 61 in 1899 had increased to 168 by 1905. Mary Lily was soon to put herself forward for another onerous task.

Lily was elected as Parish Councillor in November 1901 along with Agnes Husband. They were the first two women to be elected in Dundee. Until 1894, and the passing of the Local Government Scotland Act, women were disqualified from standing, but changes in Scottish Poor Law administration altered this situation. This did not come without opposition, and much of the most vehement dissent came from other women. Some felt it was work that *no lady would dream of doing*, whilst others thought the kind of woman who would enter this arena would live such an uninteresting existence that she would be unrepresentative of popular views.[142] Whatever her motivations for entering a committee environment which had always been populated entirely by men (and still had a great majority of males on its benches) Mary Lily Walker was proving to herself yet again that she could overcome her shy nature and gentle sensibilities. Her campaign pitch was based on the value of having women representing domestic issues; asking the rhetorical question *were there no matters which could be dealt there by women to women?*[143]

The reception faced by Agnes and Lily was not one of open-armed welcome and the women were made to feel as pariahs, but there was hardly accord amongst the men either. The points that Lily would have wanted to raise were ignored, and the conditions and welfare of the poor, the expected agenda of a Parish Council, were regularly absent from debate. Agnes Husband did manage to force through an idea to introduce the Brabazon Employment Scheme into the Poorhouse in Dundee, which was an endeavour that Lily picked up on for uses in the DSU. Mary Jane Brabazon, Countess of Meath in Ireland, had established an idea to get asylum inmates to do craft work, and to sell the produce in order to buy more materials.[144] This self-perpetuating scheme seemed an excellent idea for clubs and for poorhouse inmates. The other scheme taken on board by the DSU around the same time was something else suggested by Lily. This was inspired by a scheme in London, and in 1902, along with a Brabazon Committee, the DSU promoted the Invalid Children's Aid Association. This was a very successful initiative, and it was also very popular amongst volunteers, particularly middle-class women volunteers, who viewed the work with handicapped children as being preferably to the more daunting rent-collecting role.[145]

Mary Lily Walker was, by the early 1900s, very much the driving force behind DSU, but she still felt the need to gentle any ideas past the various committees. One such idea was the imperative in recruiting professional help, rather than sticking to the tried, and sometimes sorely tested, volunteer system. She encouraged friends and colleagues she had met through her London experience to come to Dundee 'to take up the work of the Union'.[146] Effecting these changes called for tact and diplomacy at times, and, at other times, unveiled threats to sever her ties. She used this method to persuade the DSU to help finance a scheme to train workers at Grey Lodge, the home she owned in Wellington Street in Dundee.

This was a very different approach from that formerly used by Lily. She was maturing (she was 40 in 1903) and would have the sense which experience singularly brings, but she also managed to exude a confidence and assuredness that, although bolstered by her faith, was not in keeping with her nature. The DSU saw the better of sense and fully accepted Lily's proposal. Grey Lodge took in "grey" lodgers in the shape of people like Rhoda Bethell and Miss Picot. It became the fourth settlement house to be established in Scotland but it was unique in the way it was not directly connected to a university, a factor that would be important in its long-term sustainability.[147]

The growing success of the DSU did not go unnoticed, and neither did the tireless work of Mary Lily. The DSU had been faltering, but through her drive and determination it began to regain its sense of purpose and its reputation. The most important thing she did was to bring the attention back to the individuals who were as desperately in need of help as they had ever been. It was a matter of people, not of concepts; it was a matter of giving yourself, to and for them. Whilst giving evidence along with Lily to the Poor Law Commisioners, Isobel Carlaw-Martin, who was a member of the Dundee School Board, and also of the DSU, told them:

> *Miss Walker is very modest in what she said about the Social Union. She really started it herself, and she has found it uphill work in getting workers. She has now educated public opinion to a certain extent, and we have a larger body of workers than we ever have had.*

The middle years of the first decade of the twentieth century brought many changes to the life of Mary Lily. In 1904, on 10th April, John Duff Bruce, husband to her half-sister Eliza, died of cardiac failure at Sunnybank. John Bruce was a member of the committee of the Women's Hospital, where he had supported Lily and her ideas emphatically. He was a link to the past in many ways; he had been her father's partner, and Thomas's will showed that Bruce had been asked to pay £350 for that privilege. His was the only Walker family wedding that Lily had ever been to, and he had been the man of the family in the absence of her brother Arthur, who had been gone and deliberately out of touch for what seemed an age. Mary Lily must have felt sorry for Eliza losing her husband in such a way. His service was at St Peter's Church in Perth Road, and his cortege travelled directly to the Western Cemetery where he was interred alongside Thomas, and Anna Louisa, awaiting the moment when his wife would join him again and complete the six lairs of the plot. For some reason, his name rarely appeared in census reports, and neither did he always receive a mention in Dundee Postal Directories prior to becoming Thomas's partner. His will has proved impossible to track down and there was never a mention of him paying the agreed money to join Thomas. John Duff Bruce was a good deal younger than Eliza, and he died eight years before she did. His nephew registered his death and closed the door on an interesting yet curious life.

At the November election in the same year, Agnes Husband lost her seat on the Parish Council. Lily was now the only woman amongst a group of twenty-nine men. Between January and August 1905, Lily rarely attended the council meetings, partly because of the exhausting work she had taken on in drawing up the Dundee Social Union Report with Mona Wilson. But it was also because her brother had died on the 10th of February that year.

With Arthur at his deathbed, in Carr Hill, Gateshead, had been a nurse and a housekeeper, and no one else. He had lived the life of a recluse for several years and died in exactly the same way. His nature had been the opposite of his sister's; where she was caring, and loving and considerate, he seemed cold and unable or unwilling to make friends, apart from one Albert Periam Pyne. Mary Lily must have fretted after her brother in the early days, and no doubt at family anniversaries and Christmases he was remembered, but his disappearance from sight was probably accompanied by a diminishing regularity of thought in the minds of his sisters. His body was brought up by train to Dundee, and he was buried in the family grave beside his mother, the woman who gave him life to satisfy the wishes of her husband, and who may very well have suffered her deteriorating physical condition as a consequence.

By September 1905 Mary Lily had returned to council duties, and had been chosen as a representative to the Distress Committee, a newly-formed extension to the council. A 'Memorandum on the Census of Paupers in Scotland', which was released in March 1906, showed the number of men, women and children who were most in need of Poor Relief. There were 39,782 women listed, and only 16,440 men, whilst the number of boys and girls were roughly equal at 19,000 each. These figures confirmed what Lily already knew, and what kept her resolve constant; that women and children were the real sufferers in every way amongst the poorest and most deprived communities. She recommended to the council that a Female Assistant Inspector be installed to supervise the care and support of female and children paupers. Her peers roundly rejected this.[148]

On October 30th 1907, weeks before the Parish Council elections, Mary Lily's half-sister, Grace, died from the effects of gastro enteritis from which she had suffered for two days. Dr Emily Thomson, who was a dear friend of Lily and one of the medical officers at the Women's Hospital, attended Grace and duly signed the death certificate. She died at Sunnybank, which she'd shared with Eliza, the house that had been Grace's home for forty years and more. Losing her was very sad; Grace was the rock that had always been there for Lily. She was the quiet one, always on hand if needed and happy to play a supporting role when called upon. Grace had been nearest to Lily in age, albeit almost thirty years older, and Grace had been the one who had matriculated along with Lily in the distant days when University College had first opened. She had been at the wedding between Thomas and Mary Anne, down in Kirkby Lonsdale, where she'd signed the certificate along with Hector Turnbull, who had witnessed the marriage.

Hector Turnbull had died in 1905, at his home in Hill Street, Broughty Ferry, at the age of 87. Hector was the son of Thomas Walker's sister, Jacobina Margaret, and his calendering business, in Dundee's St Andrews Street, was directly behind Thomas's office in Seagate. The Turnbulls had marriage and business connections to the Sandeman dynasty in Perth, and to the Walkers of Dundee. He would have been there to support Thomas's family as much as he could, something that families did well in Victorian times.

Grace was 73 when she passed away with both Eliza and Mary Lily by her bedside. She had lived that long life by "private means" and her will confirmed her financial well-being. Grace "gave of herself" in the more old-fashioned way; by being on the Ladies Committee of charitable institutions or on the jumble sale stall at YWCA fetes. Grace's will named a plethora of charities and institutions that would benefit from her bequests. Mary Lily was Trustee for Grace, and must have stifled a smile at the wholly appropriate but very predictably random recipients from the will. The YWCA, which had enjoyed a lot of Grace's time, was left just £5, whilst the China Inland Mission Office in London was given £500, and the Dundee & District Rescue Home benefited to the tune of £30, while the Mildinary Mission to the Jews received £200.

She left money to children who had been named after her (her *'name-daughters'* as she termed them) and to neighbours, but the main bequests went to religious societies of different faiths, to foreign missions for aid work and to local charitable organisations. Her main estate went to Mary Lily, though Eliza was to have life-rent on the estate during the remainder of her lifetime. In many ways, Grace epitomised the Victorian ideal of charitable giving more than any other in the family. Her heart ruled her head, but only as far as social convention would let it. No letters from Grace have come to light, but she is mentioned in several letters of others, and always she seemed to be busying herself for that collection or this charity. Lily missed Grace, but must have harboured poignant thoughts when Grace was buried in the family plot at Balgay Hill beside her brother and mother. At least the three of them were resting together.

The highs and lows of life continued for Mary Lily, and her workload increased. The holidays away, often with the Petersons in Alassio but sometimes with friends like Rhoda and Mona, were more necessary than ever to keep her body and soul together. There was much going on in social work in England, particularly in London, and the Liberal government were manifestly departing the old laissez faire style of politics and heralding plans for state controlled social reforms. This pleased Lily enormously. Always she felt that those who run affairs, whether they were municipal bodies or the state, should be contributing to, and reinforcing, the sterling work of disparate reformers and social work volunteers across the country. Now ideas on school meals and medical inspections for children were becoming realities, even if Dundee Council's reputation for tardiness and procrastination meant it was usually a step behind other cities and towns. Pensions for the elderly were being mooted, as were labour exchanges for the unemployed, and national and health insurance for some categories of workers. Even maternity benefits for women were being considered. This was manna from Heaven as far as she was considered, and the shy lady from Dundee, bedecked in grey habit, threw herself into all that she could manage. She was wise enough not to abandon social life of a sort, and to maintain friendships, but these had time only to be a part of her days.[149]

The 1907 elections in November meant that she was joined on the Parish Council by three other ladies, one of whom was Dr Alice Moorhead, a dear friend and colleague from the Women's Hospital where Mary Lily's role as secretary was operating very well. Immediately Moorhead unearthed some chicanery at the West Poorhouse, where records were largely unwritten, and for good reason.[150] When compared to the town's other poorhouse, the "West" was costing more and apparently providing less. Her fellow councillors, some of the men, at least seemed unperturbed and even critical of this *find*. This was Dundee after all: a city that, since the late-eighteenth/early-nineteenth century tenure of Provost Alexander Riddoch, tended to foist ironic respect on those who had fiddled the system.[151]

The Grey Lodge was moving in the direction that Lily hoped it would, and the training of women meant that she had up to six boarders partly financed by Dundee Social Union who would be helping in the running of things and involving themselves in the Union's housing department and in other areas of social work. Lily's constant intention for the settlement was to work along with municipal authorities. An article in the *Dundee Advertiser* of 1st March explained that Grey Lodge strove to help with *Public Health issues, with the School Board, and with the Poor-law*. At this time, the work of the DSU was being mentioned in the House of Commons, and the disturbing statistics which Mary Lily's work was providing fuelled the debates.[152]

Despite the revitalisation of DSU, and its emergence as a real force for social reform, there was occasional friction amongst committee members. Mary Lily was the only woman on the Executive Committee, and the only one in business meetings, but her proactive style and the fact that she was shaping its continued development did not go down well with all executive members. Professor Stegall, once her lecturer and tutor at university, took less kindly to the way things were being carried out, but his 'Victorian views on the world' were shouted down by D'Arcy Thompson and Alexander MacKay, who was then President of the Union. The Housing Department, once the only area which made substantial progress, was no longer growing, and the emphasis, through Lily's direction, was geared towards maternal and child welfare.[153] Quiet, mild, Mary Lily Walker was, by utter necessity, overruling people like Stegall, something she once could not have dreamed of. But more than that she was criticising the archaic systems that were holding back progress.

She attended the Royal Commission on the Poor Laws, where her evidence was critical of the Dundee Parish Council. She felt it was 'the duty of the Parish Council to give sufficient aliment to keep body and soul together'. This was particularly the case for relief of the elderly and widows with children. But her diatribe did not stop at Dundee's doorstep, for she also criticised the Scottish system of Poor Law administration because it precluded the sick wives and children of able-bodied men, bringing 'a great deal of hardship and suffering'. Her next volley at 'the system' was aimed at 'hard and rigid officialism':

> The officials have no time, and the councillors do not come into contact with the poor; there might be more personal, friendly care of the aged pensioners and of the boarded-out children.[154]

She had time because she made time, and she came into constant contact with the poor and elderly. Her final complaint to the Royal Commission was on the subject of the dearth of women inspectors. She concluded that, *'When so many of the problems are connected with women and children, the employment of some women inspectors might be fraught with great benefit'.* This last complaint achieved no success.[155]

In 1905, the Unemployed Workmen's Act saw a Dundee Distress Committee formed. The ethos behind the Act was to provide relief work for skilled, temporarily unemployed men to save them coming under the Poor Law and prevent any stigma. The Conservatives tried to exclude Scotland from this, citing the cost, but it did eventually cover all workmen. Its existence was short-lived; the Liberals inherited it from a departing Conservative government and had ideas of their own to promote.[156] Mary Lily embraced the idea, and became Chairwoman of the Dundee Distress Committee. For the next two years she dutifully turned up for weekly meetings at the Labour Exchange and assessed applicants for relief. Anyone receiving "a ticket" was entitled to work, either at constructing sewers, or cleaning streets, or even breaking stones, and the rate of pay was five old pennies per hour. The scheme withered away eventually, for lack of government funding and voluntary contributions.[157]

The Liberal government passed the National Health Insurance Act in December 1911, which was designed to provide sickness and unemployment insurance to workers in three specific industries. This was to be funded by contributions from the employee, the employer and the state. Wives of those insured were eligible for a maternity benefit of one pound ten shillings, and the Scottish Insurance Commission was appointed to bring the Act into play. Mary Paterson was a serving Commissioner, and Mary Lily became actively involved as a member of the

Sanatorium Benefit Committee and Convenor of the Medical Benefit committee.[158] This work, and the Act itself, appealed greatly to Lily, who saw it as *the great step forward in social legislation its promoters intended it to be*. Commissioner Mary Paterson, who would become a true friend to Lily, and also a trustee of her will, remembered Lily's efforts:

> she set herself to explain and "popularise" it among the working women in Dundee. As a member of the Insurance Committee there ... she rendered great service. Her letters to me, during the year and a half of the Acts, before her death, were, at times, almost daily events, and I am glad she lived to see some of the women for whom she cared so much benefitting from the medical attendance and the payments secured to them as a right by the Act.[159]

Lily became the last surviving member of Thomas Walker's family on the 19th of March 1912 when Eliza passed away. The register showed she was 84, making her by far the longest-lived of the family. In becoming Mrs John Duff Bruce, Eliza was the only one of the ten children to marry. They had no children, which made Mary Lily her sole surviving blood relative. Her death certificate was made out by Dr A M Stalker, who was her family doctor and had certified the death of her husband eight years earlier. She died of Broncho-pneumonia, from which she had been suffering for five days. The weather in Dundee in April of that year had been unseasonably cold with *flurry after flurry of icy precipitation*,[160] and it can be imagined that this may have speeded the end of a very long life by any standard. Lily registered the death the following day and, interestingly, she noted that Eliza's husband had been a *solicitor before the Supreme Court*. Lily was present at Eliza's death.

Eliza's will, as might be expected, saw the bulk of her estate left to her last sister, but she did, just as Grace had, leave bequests to a few others. The Church had always played a big part in her life, and almost from its completion in the 1840s she had been a member of St Peter's Free Church in Dundee's Perth Road. She left the Minister, Rev Alexander White, £500, and his daughter May received £100, as did the Deacon's Court of St Peters for sustentation work. She gave another £100 to the cleaning and improvement of the church, and some members of the congregation were bequeathed the same amount. She gave money to the Scottish Coast Mission, to the British Society London, and to Bernardo's Homes for their charitable works. Like Grace, she left money to a name-daughter, Eliza Graham, who was daughter of a mill-worker in Dundee's Taylors Lane. She also left £20 to each of the two servants in her employ, amongst a sprinkling of other small bequests.[161]

Eliza was very different to Grace. She may well have been more rebellious and more accustomed to challenging convention. Like Grace, she lived by the *private means* administered by her father, but there were times in her life when she seems to have taken her own course. Whether she was happy when her father decided to marry again is unclear, and whether his new wife being roughly the same age as herself was awkward and even embarrassing is not known either. Almost certainly Eliza did not go to her father's second wedding, which may point to discord. Eliza's position in the household would have changed with the arrival of Mary Anne. Eliza's place as the "woman of the house" would have started on the death of her Aunt Jean in 1861, but would have ended with the arrival of her father's new bride in late 1862. In Thomas's absences, and these must presumably have been many in his courting of Mary Anne Allen from Kirkby Lonsdale, she would have dictated the pace of the house, entertained as far as she had to, and made sure the servants were up to their duties. Eliza, of course, was not the oldest child of Thomas's (Anna Louisa was older by two years than her stepmother-to-be) but Anna's condition meant that the senior role came to Eliza.

Further example of Eliza's independent mind was her marriage. Her husband was six years younger than she was, and this was an unusual, though certainly not unique, situation in middle-class society. Despite being a member of the Free Church of Scotland, and a regular at St Peter's Church where William McGonagall also worshipped, she married in the Church of England. The venue was in Lytham, Lancashire, a town that was served by the railway and would later flourish as a tourist destination. Both Grace and Lily had been bridesmaids, so any thoughts of Eliza "running off" to get married were unfounded. Eliza had been a member of the Ladies Committee for a few charitable organisations in Dundee before she married, but kept almost all of these arrangements afterwards too. Her membership of the Royal Orphanage lapsed when they moved premises to the Ferry Road in the east of Dundee, so her charitable spirit tended to be constricted by geography. A few letters to Mary Lily remain where the sort of existence Eliza lived in was revealed.

My dearest Lily

We were very glad to get your card to-day – but I felt quite vexed I had not given you more lunch. However you would both be refreshed by Uncle's provisions.

Grace was at three meetings today & finished off by being at old Lady Easy's to dinner. I had three callers today to intertain but being all good talkers the effort was not great Miss Bela & her German friend & Mrs Mackieson. Was awfully glad to hear of your presentation as you had had so much to do unaided. Grace was collecting at Mrs Fraenkls to day.

I saw Bessie yesterday another letter from Malcolm telling that Willie Sandeman has come out of hospital and gone to lodgings.

Waiting for Maggie's arrival. The cold is intense to day east wind sharp peoples noses either blue or white.

I hope you will really rest & come home better for you did look for a few days back terribly tired out. Monday is the peoples Holiday I want John to go somewhere he is not quite the thing very tired & not eating – I don't know if he will budge he does not seem inclined as he is in the midst of property sales & worry

Grace & he send love and with the same

Your affect. Sister
Eliza

Remembrances to Mater & Uncle[162]

The letter indicates that Eliza viewed the world from her living room, and that although sister Grace was running about, visiting and collecting for charity, she *'intertained'* instead. Mention of Lily's presentation would refer to prize-giving at the University, and this letter must have been to the address of James Allen, where Lily and her *'mater'* would be staying. Husband John was obviously working hard, especially in property sales, and all in all it is the letter of a Victorian lady immersed in her domesticity and social setting. It was probably written around 1886.[163] A second letter from Eliza, again without a date but probably from the early 1900s, again describes the introverted world Eliza existed in:[164]

My dearest Lily

What a lovely bag it comes into immediate use via the sewing Room for my work – I was glad to get your letter & see where your holidaying? – I hope you will have fine weather & enjoy yourselves & you get a lot of sleep.

Mrs Carnegey remembers quite well of Mr & Mrs Thomson a daughter who was to be married but she does not remember of a child as Dr Emily she supposed was there. I hope you are feeling stronger

Tennant only left us to day he seemed to have enjoyed himself, he had been great with George Miller.

Have the Pewtersons gone to Jedburgh & your Grace also & the Cat & kittens – Are they to be all the Month & do you join them at the end of the month? – the letters now sent came a few days ago but we did not know where to send them …

Grace was at the Ferry today, Beth & Kate are great friends.

Kate looking ill and thin, Aunt Bessie's breathing bad. So one would think things won't be long now – remember me to Dr Emily I do hope you will both have a very enjoyable time at Laggan

And with much love
Ever dearest Lily
Your loving sister
Eliza

Eliza was buried on the 21st March 1912 in the same plot as her husband, her father and her sister Anna Louisa.

The first dozen years had been very productive and very active for Mary Lily. She had served on numerous committees and introduced several initiatives designed to improve the lives of as many of Dundee's citizens, particularly women and children, as she could. Her social work was entirely guided by the fact that she visited, and understood as much as she could, the poor and the destitute. She had to combat her own reserved sensibilities in order to be as effective as she could. One letter, which came from D'Arcy Thompson's wife, revealed how much Lily was unique in her selfless giving herself:[165]

Gowrie College   *Oct 13th [no year]*

Dear Lily

Thanks so much for your card. I shall be very glad to come to the meeting on the 22nd but I'm afraid I must refuse being on the Committee this year although I should like to be.

There seems so much to do and I 'Knock up so easily'; this last week I had neuralgia again and today is the first day I have felt well.

I want to see you, to hear all you are doing & did while we were away. I hope you weren't too busy on Tuesday week to talk a little to me

With love
Yours affectionately
Maureen Thompson

Maureen Thompson's appearance on the scene must have had some impact on the very personal relationship that Lily had enjoyed with D'Arcy. In the perfect Victorian melodrama they would have wed, despite all the obstructions and family problems that got in the way. In real life they didn't, possibly because neither was bold enough to make the first step, but Lily's move to deeper faith after the death of Madge Valentine, and her admission that she valued her love for Madge above that for him, seemed to spell the end of the "romance" for D'Arcy. Lily saw it differently, and may well have thought that more profound faith would lead to a more profound, and ultimately shared, relationship. The above letter, from the woman who did marry him, shows the difference in the physical and emotional sides between each of the women. Lily would have been reluctant to turn down committee membership for any reason. Maureen did, but may have been quite ill to have complained about her ailments in such a way. Would Lily have thought as much of herself?

Chapter 6

The 1912 Overtures

The British Association for the Advancement of Science came back to Dundee to hold its annual meeting in 1912; a full forty-five years after their first visit, an event which had done so much to change the life of the city. Along with quite a few people, many from its burgeoning further education establishment, D'Arcy Wentworth Thompson was very keen to have the highly successful meeting of 1867 repeated. The council warmed to the idea and a public meeting to discuss the matter was held in March 1910. It met with approval, and plans were quickly set into motion to make the second meeting as successful as the first had been. Whereas the earlier meeting had no accompanying booklet, apart from the British Association's own agenda and timetable, it was decided that a booklet should be made available to each of the delegates and members of the Association who came to Dundee for their eighty-second annual meeting. This would come to be recognised as the group's most successful meeting ever, with the highest number of ticket sales in the history of their annual meetings. It was also notable for the donation of £10,000 made by local businessman and jute magnate, James Caird.[166]

The executive committee which included the Lord Provost, the Town Clerk, the Chairman of Dundee's Chamber of Commerce and University College's Professor D'Arcy Thompson, made the trip to the 1910 meeting at Sheffield, and their enthusiastic invite to the Association to bring the 1912 meeting to Dundee was accepted. The booklet printed for the event was more meaningfully described as a book, for it ran to 683 pages. It contained a history of Dundee and a list of the current services and facilities. It also looked at the town's industrial successes and educational provisions, as well its scientific and cultural developments. There were articles written on a variety of topics by invited people. The articles required the contribution of seventy-five people with different areas of expertise – but only two of them were women. Mary Lily Walker wrote 'Work among Women', whilst Miss A S Maxwell wrote about Dundee *as a shopping centre*.[167]

The section on Dundee hospitals was penned by the Medical Officer for Health, Chas Templeman MD DFSc, who also wrote the article on public health in the city of Dundee. In the Dundee hospitals section, he made mention of the Women's Hospital, which he termed *The Private Hospital for Women*. This hospital began its existence as a small Clinic and Dispensary for women in the Hilltown area of the town before moving to 19 Seafield Road, a street off the Perth Road. It was seen by Templeman as offering a vital service to women.

The article tells of a committee set up in 1896 to provide a service whereby women of the town could be treated by women medical practitioners. Although set up to treat *patients suffering from those diseases peculiar to women* it was noted that women with any other ailments requiring special treatment might also be treated. This facility, wrote Templeman, was ideal for those who could not afford treatment at private hospitals, but who would *shrink away* from treatment at general hospitals. The hospital was funded to a degree by voluntary contributions, and patients might be expected to pay *between ten shillings and one guinea per week'.* Apparently this charge would be waived in special circumstances. The article noted that the hospital was about to move to *'high ground overlooking the river'* (Elliott Road), and that an unnamed lady *'belonging to the city'* had a deep interest in the hospital, had generously given funds for the new building, and had been on the original committee. Mrs F B Sharp had generously given much of the funding but the unnamed lady was Mary Lily Walker who, along with with Doctors Emily Thomson and Alice Moorhead, had provided a sensitive and necessary facility for needy women.[168]

Committees of management were important institutions in Victorian and Edwardian times, and the Women's Hospital was no exception. Its 1896 constitution required that *'it shall consist of not less than 12 and not more than 21 members, 7 of whom shall retire annually, but shall be eligible for re-election'.* Amongst these committee members were Mary Lily Walker, her brother-in-law John Duff Bruce, and her friend and mentor D'Arcy Wentworth Thompson. The first annual meeting was held on June 21st 1897, and it reported that in the year since it opened on May 1st 1896, at total of forty-one women had been admitted, of whom thirty-eight came under the attention of the medical officers. Of these women, thirty-two were cured, five had symptom relief, and one had sadly died of an *'advanced cancerous disease'.* Miss M L Walker attended, as did Mr John Duff Bruce, but D'Arcy Thompson was away on a field trip to the Bering Straits at the time. Rules which had been laid out for in-patients were continued and read as follows:

1. *Patients coming into Hospital are required to bring a change of linen, comb, brush, towel and soap for their own use.*

2. *They are required to provide themselves with clean linen twice a week. Patients' linen can be sent to the laundry at their own expense, if they desire it.*

3. *No wine, spirits, or food is allowed to be brought into the Hospital by patients or their friends, except by permission of Medical Officers.*

4. *All charges are payable in advance.*

5. *Visitors to patients are admitted on: Wednesdays 6.30–7.30, Sats & Sundays 3.00–4.00.*

A new wing was added to the building in 1900, and was officially opened at the annual meeting of subscribers on 27th December of that year. In anticipation of the move to Elliott Road, Dr Templeman, in the 1912 handbook, used the euphemisms in keeping with the sensibilities of the time when he said that the new Women's Hospital would be equipped with *'all modern appliances for the treatment of that class of diseases it is especially designed to deal with'.*[169]

An ex-magistrate of Dundee, Mr J H Martin, JP, wrote in the handbook about the *'present state'* of Dundee in 1912, and he used many comparisons to the town when the British Association was last there. Whereas there were virtually no sewers in 1867, there were now ninety-eight miles of these, which he claimed had done much to save the city from the *'ravages of disease and epidemic'* that had previously been so prevalent. He commented also on the number of streets in the town; there were now 648 in the city of which 305, covering thirty-two miles, had been constructed since 1867. There was an almost unlimited supply of fresh water, compared with the very few wells known for their doubtful purity, and the baths and wash-houses that were providing an aggregate of over 450,000 visits per year. This may not amount to a huge number per person per annum when the population in 1911's census was 165,000, but it was a provision which simply was not available to the 104,000 inhabitants of Dundee in 1867. Martin also lauded the *'enlightened methods applied to the cleansing of the city'*, but, in truth, even the slightest improvement would have been immeasurably better than the conditions before. He did mention that a higher tone of hygiene had been achieved in *'nearly'* every class of Dundee's community, and then commented on housing in the city, where he insisted that *'earnest efforts are still being made to reconstruct ... the still backward parts of the city'*.

The *'still backward parts of the city'* included some of the homes condemned in Mary Lily Walker's 1905 Social Report as being unfit for purpose, and in most cases, unfit for any purpose. But the Dundee of 1912 was very different to the 1867 version. Dundee was elevated to the status of *'county of a city'* in 1892, which heightened civic pride but had probably more to do with commercial and industrial successes than its rapid improvement in housing stock. Some areas had undergone great changes, including the Commercial Street area where a clutter of medieval housing had been razed to the ground. Murraygate and Seagate too had seen buildings disappear and re-emerge, whilst great changes were made to the thoroughfare leading from the bottom of the Hilltown to the foot of Dens Road. What had previously been Bucklemaker Wynd, named by James Soutar as *'about the dirtiest place imaginable in the universe'*, was now the *'much wider and considerably less steep'* Victoria Road. These developments, however, were possibly less to do with providing new dwellings to replace old, and much more to do with providing a much gentler slope for horse-drawn carts to pull raw jute from dock to mill. The new buildings which sprang up on either side of these improved streets did, however, do a lot to improve the façade and to make the centre of the *'city'* a nicer place. Improvements in the Seagate would continue until the premises where Thomas Walker, and later John Duff Bruce, had plied their profession as solicitors, which no longer existed.

The improvements in housing which had been welcomed in the mid-1870s through to the 1890s began to stutter to a halt going into the twentieth century, mainly due to an escalation of costs for building materials. In 1900 there were a number of outbreaks of infectious diseases. Areas with chronic overcrowding and poor sanitation, such as Overgate, Blackness Road, Foundry Lane and Middle Street, were predictably badly affected, but ironically the area around Hilltown, which had had some of its housing rebuilt, suffered most of the problems and incurred most of the deaths. It was estimated in 1901 that *'one third of the citizens of Dundee had either poor, or no, sanitary convenience'.*

The Dundee Postal Directory of 1908 revealed that there were fewer Irish-sounding names in Dundee than there had been forty years earlier, possibly as a result of Irish women marrying into local families and taking their surnames. In their place there appeared quite a number of a few Italian names. The O'Haras and the Coonans were replaced by the Franchis and the Gallozzis, and these Italian immigrants, with their fish and chip shops and ice-cream parlours, would soon promote local concern. These establishments sold their wares well into the evening, and even opened on Sundays. This incurred the ire of locals who complained about local youngsters congregating around such places and causing disturbances. These complaints, which promoted some trouble between the Italian community and affected locals, came at just the time when the Dundee Handbook was describing a diminution in the number of crimes due to *'a great advance in the sobriety of living'*, and boasting of court sessions where there were no cases to try. Apparently, in twenty-five years of court records in Dundee there had been eight "maiden" sittings with no cases, and four of them had been in the eighteen months to 1912.[170]

Whilst court cases were apparently diminishing, and drunkenness appeared not to be as bad as it had been in the past, there was still much to be done in the care of children in Dundee. The 1912 handbook contained a section entitled 'The Care of the Children' where Jas Younger, MB, CM, spelled out the problems still facing the city. His opening lines were hard-hitting and condemnatory, in a similar manner to that which Mary Lily Walker had expressed in her talk to DSU members in 1899. He began:

> *This subject may be viewed from the two aspects of sentiment or hard fact. The sentimentalist becomes a subscriber to a charitable organisation, and is rewarded once a year by the gift of a more or less voluminous Report, and, ensconced in his armchair before the fire, he is able with ill-conceived pride, to view his name in large type opposite his modest donation, and there his responsibility ends. The observer of hard fact on the other hand is also a subscriber and receives the same document, but, in dipping his hand into his pocket, he spares neither time nor personal effort in trying to better the condition of the children. We know full well that, in spite of improved sanitation and social conditions, infant mortality is abnormally high compared with that of adults.*

This attack on casual philanthropy, where money, rather than "self" is given, chimed exactly with the message the DSU and Mary Lily had been promoting, and the picture painted of the money-giver conceitedly eyeing his name and his donation on a Report was exactly the one that Lily felt needed to be addressed.

Younger went on to attack many aspects which impacted on the health of children. He attacked the *'influences of parental unfitness, alcoholism and industrial employment of women'*, which brought grave social problems as yet unsolved. He condemned the large number of parents who were quite simply physically or mentally unfit to have children because any such offspring could hardly be expected to remain healthy.

He railed at "experts" who failed to see that the circulation of alcohol in the maternal blood must reach and affect the unborn child, injuring tissue or stopping cell development, and effectively *bringing about its death*. He chided that the byproducts of alcohol were *crime, social degradation and child neglect*; that the problem should not be underestimated and that the blame for the *huge infant mortality, stunted physique and dwarfed mentality of so many surviving children* could, for the large part, be blamed on the abuses of alcohol.

The situation, peculiar to Dundee, of married women having to work immediately before and very soon after giving birth, was also an influence in child mortality. Sir John Simon (1816–1904) was the first medical officer of health to the City of London (1848–55) and also fulfilled this role for central government from 1855 to 1876. In this capacity he created public health legislation which resulted in the Sanitary Act of 1866. His investigations into adult women performing factory or agricultural work showed that infant mortality increased in these cases. The findings of Chas Templeman, Medical Officer for Health in Dundee, mirrored those of Simon, but in Dundee other factors made the situation markedly worse. The Factory Acts had unequivocally stipulated that nursing mothers should not return to work until at least one month after delivery. This was flouted in Dundee. Very young infants were often looked after whilst their mothers worked. Between taking children out in the cold air, and the feeding of children from dirty bottles or even *scraps from the table*, the risk of illness can be understood. Infant health, according to Younger, *depends far more on infant rearing than on the physical condition of the parents, the sanitation of the houses, or even poverty*.

All of these things would have had the full agreement of the Dundee Social Union, and in the 1912 handbook Younger praised that body for their efforts. He particularly approved of the *'restaurants for nursing mothers'* scheme, which he claimed, by feeding under-fed mothers, enriched their milk for breast feeding. This initiative was entirely thought up and put into action by Mary Lily Walker, and such was her earnestness about the scheme working that she went to Paris to observe a similar idea of Madame Henri Coullet's in action. Lily anonymously described herself as *'a public spirited citizen'* for financing the nursing mother's restaurants, rather than accept any praise.

Mary Lily's own contribution to the splendid 1912 handbook was entitled 'Work among Women', and it provided some fascinating and alarming facts, covering eight pages of the publication. It was written as a narrative, but her points provided a list of data:

1. *There were 9 women to every 7 men in Dundee;*

2. *Dundee had the largest proportion of women householders in Scotland at 33%;*

3. *Between the ages of 20 to 44 there were 3 women for every 2 men;*

4. *15,000 out of 30,000 women in that age group were unmarried;*

5. *Dundee had 23.4% of its married women in work, Edinburgh and Glasgow had just over 5% each;*

6. *Of 34,400 employed in textile manufacture, only 23% were men over twenty-three years of age;*

7. *The jute industry relied mainly on the labour of women, girls and lads;*

8. *Weavers and winders are considered a hard-working, self-respecting class;*

9. *Spinning and preparing mills employ most of the married women with children;*

10. *Dundee has an over-employment of women and an under-employment of men;*

11. *Dundee has the highest infant death rate, high illegitimacy and greatest poverty;*

12. *Dundee women were more concerned with insurance for funerals than sickness;*

13. *There are 10,000 women members of Burial Societies.*

From this string of facts, Lily provided a background into the situation for working women in Dundee. The document gave many examples of the dilemma facing women in the city. It is noticeable that the number of people employed in textiles in 1912 was five thousand fewer than in the 1905 DSU Report, and this diminution in itself explains the continuing poverty problem. The insurance for funerals also epitomises the problems of infant mortality.

Lily pointed out that the municipality, despite its sometimes tardy attitude, was as gravely concerned about high infant mortality as she was, as so many responsible people in the town were. She recounted that two lady visitors had been appointed in 1903 to visit the houses in the poorer districts, and to *'enquire into the causes of death in young children'*. The feeding of infants was thought to be of prime importance, and a woman, faced with the dilemma of staying at home to feed her newborn or going to work to earn enough to save her older children and herself from starving, often chose the latter option. These restaurants for nursing mothers were set up to directly influence this unacceptable situation. By giving cheap meals to women, Mary Lily hoped to better their own nourishment which would in turn improve the milk fed to babies. Whilst the mothers were in need of personal help, the restaurants were, primarily, seen as the best way to promote better health for children. Some desperate cases were given free meals and there were many *'desperate cases'* in Dundee. A few conditions were necessarily placed on those who took up the generous offer. Firstly, meals were only provided during the first three months of the baby's life; secondly, the infant had to be entirely breastfed; and finally, the mothers had to agree to have their babies weighed on a regular basis to gauge progress. Photographs at the time from the Restaurant set up in Temple Lane at the city's West Port show the expectant faces of children and mothers patiently at wait for opening hours, glad at the prospect of their provided meal. They also show the bare feet of many of Dundee's children.

The Early Notification of Birth Act (1907) changed the registration of births and allowed home visits to new babies to be done much more quickly. Prior to that, a parent, specifically the husband (if one existed) was permitted up to six weeks to register a birth. There was no way that authorities could visit babies, or even know of their existence, until registration. The registrar's task was to advise the Council of all new registrations and that initiated the visits by the appointed ladies to homes with new babies. After the 1907 Act, problems were spotted much quicker by these visitors, and suitable advice and help could consequently be given. This Act thus improved the mortality rate, and in The House of Lords on 15th July 1915, Lord Hylton told the House of how much matters had improved. He mentioned 'one place' (he didn't name it but he was referring to Dundee) which had once suffered infant mortality figures of 194 out of a 1000 children, but, he was glad to relay, that the 'general rate all over the country was now 130 per 1,000'.[171] In truth, places like Burnley and Dundee were still much worse than the general picture.

The success of the first Restaurant, according to Mary Lily, was quantifiable. According to her article in the Handbook, that particular area of Dundee had seen one in four children dying, whereas a Home Office enquiry in 1909 showed the same area to have an infant mortality figure of one in five. These are still well above the *'general'* picture described by Hylton, but in Dundee's worst days, there were *'dark'* areas of the town where infant mortality was higher than the town's average. The question of infanticide had been a concern in Dundee and in other deprived urban areas. In relation to her Restaurant scheme, Lily reported that, in 1909, the *'Municipality took the matter up, opened up two other restaurants in poorer districts of the town, and gave a grant to the original one'*. Mary Lily was warmed by the success of her initiative, but frustrated to realise that, whilst the causes of the plight of women and children remained in place, that the reforming work she was setting in place was of a *'palliative rather than remedial'* nature.[172]

Her article went on to mention the town's help, to the tune of a grant for £100, towards the Dundee Day Nurseries, of which she noted there were four. These catered for around 120 children and infants, and opened early enough to accept those delivered at 5.30am by mothers heading for the usual 6.00am start. Lily bemoaned the fact that these children were lifted from warm cots and beds and taken, often in freezing conditions, to nurseries. Whilst the nurseries were well-attended, Lily was wise enough, and had her ear close enough to the ground, to realise that most mothers put their children to neighbours.

Many women in Dundee never married, and Lily mentioned the companionship that often existed when some of these women stayed in houses together. Indeed, she wrote, *'some of the most attractive houses in Dundee are those of women living as companions'*. It can be presumed she was considering the interiors of these houses as being attractive. She painted a picture of some of these women who, through living as companions, had broken free of the shackles that overcrowded, children-filled homes seemed to enforce. She had been in houses with *'drapes of muslin'* and *'beds with chintz'*, and often these types of women *'would attend lectures and classes, and take an active interest and part in Church life'* and they might even be ready to help others. Mary Lily saw that not all women needed to be anchored into the apparently inescapable morass of working class social and domestic drudgery. There was a way out for some people and women, the gender most hard-done-by in almost all ways, could take it into their own hands to take it.[173]

Not all unmarried working women found the way to self-betterment, and there was no *'central institute of girls' clubs'* to attract widespread interest.[174] There were individual committees and various halls that offered some recreational opportunities, but these seemed to have been largely spurned by this *'lower class'* of women. The YWCA, where Grace did much fundraising and other help, offered various interests, as did the Institute in Tay Street, but it was the typists, the clerks, the shop assistants and the women in business who attended these things and gained from the social and cultural exchanges.[175] The Salvation Army was often the place where these unmarried working girls and women would visit, those who were *'worsted in life's battle and have fallen out of the ranks of the steady workers'*. Or The Metropole might be where they would spend time. This was a lodging-house for the *'very poor'*, and for the *'homeless woman'*, and for the *'tramp'*, and many of its inmates met all three criteria. It accommodated 100, and inmates could cook their own food, if they had any, in a kitchen there. Soups, puddings, bread and butter and tea could all be bought there; not much protein, but sustenance to partly fill a stomach perhaps. Apparently staff members often attended Police Courts watching for potential guests whom they would do their best to help.[176]

An extended Probation System was set up to offer help and to influence women who were seen as being on the *'downward path'*. Some institutions, like the Church of Scotland and the

Catholic Church, made attempts to help, though both tended to look after women of their own faith. The Little Sisters of the Poor at their Home in Wellburn, Dundee, offered succour regardless of religious affiliations, and they could have as many as seventy-three women, some of whom had been reduced to begging *'of all kinds'* before they entered this sanctuary. Mary Lily's mother had been an active committee member of the Home for Fallen Women, in Paton's Lane, for several years, and her father had been Treasurer of the establishment. The life and the work of women, as described in her article for the 1912 handbook, could be insufferably hard, but not entirely inescapable.

At the time of the British Association meeting in 1912, Winston Churchill was the Member of Parliament for the city, a position he had held since winning a by-election four years earlier. His initial visits to Dundee did not at all impress him, or if they did it was in a very bad way. He first noted the *'crowded tenements five and six storeys high'* which were sited very close to the factories where the inhabitants worked. He felt the sound and the smell of jute manufacture would dominate the lives of these *'wretches'*. He saw families in houses where all the boys in the family slept in one room, and the girls and very often the parents too, slept in the other, which often doubled as kitchen. Usually there was a single gas light which was used for light, and for heating, and possibly even for cooking. He found the sanitation to be disgusting, or worse, and spoke of houses with *'no baths and no lavatories'*, where an open midden in the back court of the tenement was used for *'rubbish of all sorts'* and, by males, as a urinal. Women, he noted, used a pail indoors, *'emptying the contents later'*. This midden would be cleaned out weekly by Town Council "scaffies" who had to work in the darkness with only little brass paraffin lamps atop their heads for light, faking their way through their *'noisome toils'*.[177]

Churchill observed the work of the jute mill, watching the process from raw jute to *'burlap, gunny bag or carpet backing'*, and he found the hard work was being carried out by hard, dirty and unhealthy people, and he described

> *the sight then of the bobbin shifters, small boys and girls running about on bare feet covered from head to toe with white mill stoor, and harrassed bedraggled women, old before their time, tending the inexorable noisy machinery, would have angered the heart of any reformer.*[178]

And it did – it angered the heart of Mary Lily and the others engaged in the DSU.

Churchill was painting a picture of hell, at home and at work, and the picture clearly showed the people who were enduring the most hardship – the barefooted children and the bedraggled women, old before their time, who were not even afforded the decency of toilet facilities. Churchill, in witnessing these things, was probably on a conducted tour of a mill, and was probably taken to one of the better ones. This was in 1908, and this was still the situation in Dundee, a situation not very much changed from that of twenty years earlier when the DSU was formed, except by this time Dundee had lost its supremacy in jute to Calcutta. Work was less certain, and more subject to peaks and troughs, and the wages in real terms, in any terms, were lower than they had been back then.

The 1912 handbook commented on evidence of advancement in sobriety in Dundee. If that was so, then Churchill's thoughts on sobriety were somewhat different. He had already heard of Dundee's *'reputation for drunkenness'*; of the innumerable pubs where cunning owners gave free salt-fish to grateful customers who failed to understand that this was a ploy to make them thirsty and to drink all the more. He had heard of *'Dundee pay-days'*, which were Saturdays, when workers brought the night in drinking and *'brawling the length of the Overgate, and everywhere else'*, and of a police force that had *'specially-constructed wheelbarrows for carrying away the casualties'*. Winston Churchill had heard of all these things, and had steeled himself to the prospect of witnessing such things, but even so he was compelled to comment that he had *'never seen parallel to any part of the United Kingdom for such bestial drunkenness'.*[179]

These bouts of drunkenness were not restricted to men by any means, and both unmarried and married women also found solace, or at least a few hours of blissful drunken oblivion, in the depths of the beer glass or gin bottle. Children, either sitting in the stark reality of their homes, or roaming the streets for mischief or entertainment, were being brought up in a world where this situation was the norm; this was their future unveiled before their eyes, as it had been their parents' before them. This was Dundee life for very many.

One of Churchill's open-air speeches in the town, of which there were relatively few, was held in Bell Street. He stood next door to the courthouse, where not all of those who entered came out again. Opposite his vantage point was the Salvation Army Home for Fallen Women and next door to that was the Parish Council Lunatic Department. Slightly further down the road was the Night Refuge for the Homeless where vagrants could get a daytime cup of tea before setting off on their *'wanderings'*. Later, that same day, Churchill made another speech; this time indoors and to a very different Dundee audience:

> *Almost every wealthy Dundonian of any note had turned up to hear Winston and they now sat, drawn by curiosity from the plush comfort of their mansions in the fashionable West End of the city and the seaside suburb of Broughty Ferry,*

listening intently for his next thought-provoking revelation.
He paused to allow the enthusiasm of the generality of his
audience to subside.[180]

He fed his wealthy audience the rhetoric they wanted to hear.
He extolled their efforts and their *'sacrifices'*, and said that,
because people could see and appreciate just what the wealthy
of this town had done for all, that *'there is so little class hatred*
in our land in spite of all the squalor and the misery which we see
around us'. He sat down to *'tumultuous cheering and applause'*.
The sitting MP for Dundee had, in one day, seen, and been
surrounded by, all classes of life in his constituency. He was
a Liberal, and he was liberal in his praises of the *'parasites'*
described by Mary Lily Walker to the DSU. Churchill later
wrote of the evening's event:

> *I think this was upon the whole the most successful election*
> *speech I have ever made. The entire audience, over two*
> *thousand persons, escorted me, cheering and singing through*
> *the streets of Dundee to my hotel.*[181]

Churchill's candidacy for the "safe seat" of Liberal Dundee in
May of 1908 brought disputes to Dundee of a gender issue. The
Suffrage Movement, something which was already very active
in Dundee through its local Freedom League, brought many
of their most vociferous proponents to town. Churchill was
viewed as anti-feminist at least, and disturbingly misogynistic
by a few. Agnes Husband, who, along with Lily, had been one
of the first Parish Councillors in Dundee, was among those
lending a passionate voice to the meetings which Churchill
attended, as was Elizabeth Scotland from the Freedom League.
A more persistent problem at the meetings was a Miss Malony,
who carried a large hand-bell around to disturb the open-air
assemblies. There was never a mention of Mary Lily Walker
being attached to the Suffrage Movement in any way, despite
her relentless quest to secure better and fairer treatment to

that sex. Churchill was elected to Dundee despite the bell and the well-attended opposition meetings.[182]

Together with the skilled businessmen, the wealthy elite of Dundee, irrespective of how they achieved things, did thrust Dundee on to a more global stage than most other towns. Shipbuilding in Dundee, whilst dwarfed ultimately by Glasgow, was nevertheless a very renowned activity, and according to H T Templeton of the *Dundee Courier*, '*ships from Dundee could be found in every sea*'. This included ships sailing in the Arctic, a place where Dundee, for the second half of the eighteenth century and before, monopolised the whaling and seal fur industry. The textile trade meant commerce was transacted over many parts of the world, such as exported raw material from Asia, and exports of finished product to almost all parts of the Empire and many other distant places. Dundee also "exported" many very able people. Several of Dundee High School's past pupils went on to places of influence in the world with many entering the Indian Civil Service. The education provided for them was, theoretically, the same as that afforded to females, but the opportunities which accrued were definitely not. Had Thomas's wish for a son been realised, and had Mary Lily been a man, her intellect and drive, her honesty and her selflessness, would surely have allowed her to have gone very far in both the literal and metaphoric senses. Some of the sons of Dundee went to Calcutta, passing on training as well as providing machinery for the indigenous workforce. By 1912, Calcutta was seen as Dundee's '*most formidable opponent*'. The mills in Calcutta were populated by many Dundee men providing management and expertise, and millions of pounds worth of financial capital was provided by Dundee. This would have produced short-term gain for capitalists through '*good and steady*' dividends, but the gain of the few was again to result in the misery of the many. As Dundee's own jute sales began to become unsteady, wages, particularly in the early 1900s, began to suffer. This, added to the rise of Labour politics, led to strikes in Dundee. Strikes that the poverty-hit population could ill afford. Dundee's biggest export in this period might well be considered to be her people, for in the five years prior to 1912, over 10,000 Dundonians emigrated, almost certainly never to return.[183]

A good indicator of the levels of poverty and despair, and the number of institutions established and run for the amelioration of those unfortunate enough to need their help, lay in the number of such concerns. The extent of the listing of Social and Philanthropic Institutions in Dundee by 1910 was, in some ways, as depressing as it was impressive.

The Shelter was set up for children who had suffered cruelty at home, and was well-populated; it was eventually run under the auspices of the Dundee Society for the Prevention of Cruelty to Children. The Children's Free Breakfast and City Mission provided once a week meals for destitute children, whilst the Sisters of Charity at their Catholic Day Nursery in Park Place offered to do the same, as did the Boys and Girls Religious Association. Dundee Social Union ran Restaurants for Nursing Mothers, and in hard times, such as in times of "strikes", the Salvation Army and the Independent Labour Party both tried to augment this meals service. Holiday homes, where poor children might spend a few days respite away from the desperation of day-to-day life, were made available, and in this enterprise Mary Lily was one of the initiators and driving forces. The Orphanage housed an average of seventy children at a time, so the total number who passed through its doors since its inception in 1815 is incalculable, yet this establishment handled the education as well as the welfare of its inmates until 1895. The Lady Jane Ogilvy Orphanage at Baldovan and the Barnhill Orphanage also looked after many children, whilst Lawside Convent offered a home for up to twenty orphan girls at a time. The Dundee Working Boys

Home and the Society of St Vincent de Paul separately looked after destitute boys who had been ousted from their family homes. The Dundee Gospel Temperance Union and the Band of Hope, tried along with various religious organisations to put a stop to the evils of alcohol. The Juvenile Good Templar Halls and Juvenile Rechabites Tents did the same for younger imbibers. The Dundee Charitable Organisation Society acted as an umbrella operation in co-ordinating help for the poor and homeless. In 1912 it boasted of giving over £10,000 worth of help to over 28,000 destitute people in the twenty-six years of its existence. Its Curr Night Refuge in Dundee's Bell Street offered one night's accommodation to the homeless, and any one accepting this help was barred from re-visiting for a month. Almost all who returned after a month were accommodated a second time, apart from *well-known loafers or imposters'* or those who were intoxicated. There were also Sailors Homes and Homes for Ex-Prisoners. The amount of people desirous of help always exceeded the amount available in Dundee, and this level of deprivation and desperation underlines the magnitude of the task that was embarked upon by social reformers like Mary Lily Walker.[184]

The Recreation Committee was disbanded as a consequence of the poorly attended entertainments arranged by DSU, which appeared to show a lack of interest by the poorer inhabitants of Dundee in organised activities. The city did have a number of theatre venues, including Her Majesty's Theatre opened in 1885, although the Theatre Royal in Castle Street which had opened in 1810 closed for business in the same year. There were numerous concert halls, such as the Kinnaird, but these were frequented by the wealthier inhabitants of the town. By the end of the century, however, a new phenomenon, "moving pictures", began to be shown. Early examples tended to be displayed in "gaffs" or booths, or sometimes a hotel might provide the venue. In 1896, The Peoples Palace showed a film of a football match, and the Gaiety Theatre showed very occasional pieces of film at their variety theatre evenings, but again to middle class audiences. By 1910, Dundee had its first picture house when the aptly named New Cinema opened in Morgan Street. Another three were opened that same year and Dundee had thirteen by 1912. These cinemas were spread across the city, many situated in areas where the poorest lived, like Hawkhill (Hippodrome), Lochee (Nobles Picture Palace) and Well Road (Magnet Picture Palace). These were affordable, and Dundee quickly became a cinema-going community. This was a new form of escapism, a form that did not need to be alcohol-fuelled. This new entertainment soon proved itself to be a place where the working class would turn up in their masses. Yet, despite the growing popularity, the 1912 handbook made no mention of this popular new fad in its section on cultural and social activities. Yet in offering an alternative to drunkenness, the cinema proved to be no bad thing.

Different sorts of cultural activity and entertainments were extremely indicative of the class divide. The new, popular cinema fad was less likely to attract middle class patrons, more because of the sort of clientele who visited the tawdry venues that began the phenomenon. Music, that most freely available medium, became a litmus test of wealth and station. Dundee's musical acts in the last half of the nineteenth century, right up to the First World War, are of incredible world celebrity. Russian composer M. Rachmaninoff, and Englishman Sir Charles Villiers Stanford (born in Dublin) came with Mr Plunket Greene, the celebrated baritone singer. The Brussells Quartet made the long trip to perform, whilst Berlioz's 'Faust' was often performed by the Dundee Amateur Choral Union. Sir Charles Halle, founder of the world-renowned Halle Orchestra, was a regular visitor to town, as was Sir Henry Wood who had the Promenade Concerts in London renamed in his honour. Sir Arthur Sullivan, the composer forever known in the Gilbert and Sullivan operatic collaborations, came many times to watch his works, delightful in their *'intrinsic brightness, sparkle and freshness'* in Dundee's Her Majesty's Theatre. Dundee also boasted the quality of its own operatic amateurs, and the 1912 handbook mentioned that a local production of 'The Bohemian Girl' was the *'first attempt at anything approaching Grand Opera by amateurs in Scotland, if not Britain'.* That this quality of musical brilliance was coming to Dundee is indicative of the status the city had, and it also let the class divide be distinguished by the entertainment of one's taste.[185]

1912 in Dundee was also a year bedevilled by strikes. As well as serious strikes in textile factories, the *'carters and dockers'* walked out of work in December in a move that would have dreadful consequences for almost everyone in the city. Dundee was still handling much of its imported and exported goods by ship, meaning that any extended closure had knock-on effects for shops and factories.[186] Coming so soon after the six week strike of the Jute & Flax Workers Union, which began in March, the result was further poverty amongst those who most depended on their meagre wages. The strike ended in a two and a half percent increase in the wages of preparers and spinners, but it was more successful in recognising the might of the union, and in the setting up of Standing Joint Committees which would potentially avert strikes by dealing with problems before they escalated.[187] This constituted a breakthrough, and the beginnings of communication between the management of factories and their workforces. It should be noted, however, that there were more working-class people in the Dundee Burial Society, at 10,000 in 1910, than there were members of the Jute & Flax Workers Union.[188] However, it did little to change the way this industry recruited and treated its workers, nor did it address the gender imbalance. Women would continue to be the workers o' Dundee.

Chapter 7

End of Dreams

Mary Lily Walker was not a rash or spontaneous person; being the daughter of a solicitor, and becoming a scientist by academic choice, she was one to measure any situation carefully before taking action. It would seem that, for her, actions without necessary consideration were fraught and potentially harmful. That is not to say that she did not have an alert mind and a brilliant sense of imagination; the string of new initiatives and unique facilities that she thought up prove this point. It is possible, however, that her caution may have led to unfulfilled personal goals, and her relationship with D'Arcy Wentworth Thomson may well exemplify this.

By early 1913, there were some actions taken by Mary Lily that would indicate that she thought her life was coming to an end. The clearest indicator was her haste about setting her things in order and making out her last will and testimony. The detail in the will was considerable, with many beneficiaries being named. She would not have come to this final list lightly. It is easy to imagine that she must have spent many hours of lonely effort agonising on who would be in the will and the extent to which her beneficence would stretch in each and every case. This exercise would have been carried out in one of her rooms in Grey Lodge, Wellington Street, and it was a task that she undertook alone.[189]

Mary Lily would have been mindful of the hurt caused by her brother's actions, when he left his entire estate to Albert Periam Pyne. It would not have been the fact that Pyne had gained so much; Pyne was a friend, and patently a very special friend of Arthur's. If Arthur chose to leave him the estate then that was entirely his prerogative. The hurt for the Walker family was that Arthur chose to tell all who read his will that he chose, quite deliberately, to snub his family with the lines which started the official document:

> *I WISH it to be understood that the only reason why this my Will makes no provision for my relations is that those I should otherwise desire to benefit are already amply provided for.*

He left £7,887 to Pyne, who was also his sole executor, but the money would have mattered not at all to Mary Lily. What would have mattered was the odd piece from his possessions that would have represented a part of him: the small memento for her and his half-sisters that would have been special. It would not have healed the loss of love that they had long endured, but it might at least have given some emotional succour.

Plotting the start of Pyne's relationship with Arthur Walker is difficult, but they knew each other when Pyne, nine years younger than Arthur, was still a boy. At the surprisingly tender age of 16, Albert Pyne appeared in New Zealand with Arthur T J Walker. At that time, the local newspaper in Christchurch would publish the names of visitors to the town as a public interest article. In the edition of 3rd March 1892 of the Christchurch Press, it was noted that, staying at the Cokers Hotel in Christchurch, were Arthur and Albert, and it is recorded that both had sailed in from London. Cokers was a well-established Hotel, patronised by the better-off and a natural stopping-off place for tourists. The two men may also have travelled to India before going to New Zealand.[190]

Albert Pyne became a well-known man in engineering, and became a captain in the army during the First World War. His connection to Arthur is tenuous, though they did go together to New Zealand, so must presumably have met in London where Pyne studied at the City and Guilds of London Central Technical College. The only other feasible connection came when Pyne moved to Clarke Chapman & Co. They met again in Gateshead, and for a while they stayed in the same house where Pyne's wife and child were also resident. Where he was when Arthur died is unknown, but Arthur knew him well enough to leave him his entire estate, and to demonstrate his knowledge of Pyne's wife and son by naming them in the text of the will.

Arthur's will was very short and clinical in its brevity. The fact that it was witnessed by Duncan Stewart, a surgeon from Battle Hill in Hexham, and Mary Little, a Certificated Nurse from Spion Kop, again in Hexham, indicates that it was written from a sick-bed in a hospital. Arthur was described as a *reclusive invalid* at this time.[191] Arthur's will was signed and witnessed on the 9th of April 1903. It was very unusual to have such a document witnessed by a surgeon and a nurse, and it seems very reasonable to assume that the will was made out very quickly, at a time when he may have been in extreme ill health. Arthur was 38 years old when he died on the 10th February 1905 in Carr Hill House, Gateshead, a building that had once been a lunatic asylum. His body was brought up by train to Dundee[192] and he was buried in the same plot as his mother. Arthur's death and the funeral were not mentioned in the newspapers, and there is no record of Albert Periam Pyne being present. Arthur's will contained instructions about the bequest of his money; there is no mention of collected goods or furniture, neither is there a mention of leaving any keepsake to family and friends. Mary Lily would have been very conscious of not doing the same thing with her own will. She made sure she did not.

Lily's will began with a list of beneficiaries, rather than an inventory of articles and monies to be given away. Mary Lily, above all things, was a person who cared about people. Her compassion was for the children of the poor, and for their mothers who struggled against almost insuperable hardships. People were what she cared about; not statistics, not crass officialdom and obdurate bureaucracy, but people, and that included people of all classes. Her first decision in the making of the will was to choose Trustees to administer affairs and ensure her wishes were complied with.

Her cousin, John Sandeman Allen, was the first named of the Trustees. He was the son of Mary Anne's sister, Margaret, who was married to a cousin, Howard Allen.[193] John was employed as an underwriter in an insurance company, Queen Insurance, whose offices were at 11 Dale Street, Liverpool. John Allen, named after his grandfather, resided at Nunclose, Oxton, Birkenhead and had two daughters, Catherine and Frances Amy. Mary Lily's second named Trustee was her former tutor, and life-long trusted friend, D'Arcy Wentworth Thomson. His address in the will was said to be Gowrie Cottage, Barnhill, Broughty Ferry. The third Trustee was Alexander Mackay of Rock-knowe, Broughty Ferry, who was shortly to be President of the Grey Lodge Settlement, and the fourth was Miss Mary Muirhead Paterson of 11 Inverleith Terrace, Edinburgh.

The choice of Trustees would have been a relatively straightforward decision, although there must have been several others who might have entered Mary Lily's head. Her difficulty would start with deciding who was to receive something, and what to give each of those chosen. In looking at the finalised will it is easy to imagine Mary Lily Walker associating articles to people to whom they would mean something. Thinking about this would necessitate a trawl through memories, mostly precious, and always poignant. Sitting alone, with pen and paper, thinking about her own mortality and the memories of times and events with so many people who were dear to her must have been emotionally challenging. A lifetime of collected goods to be matched to a lifetime of collected friends and relatives; this must have been a bitter-sweet chore, and one that could not be hurried or curtailed. But, driven by the sense of her own impending death, Mary Lily used the same reasoning and care, and lack of spontaneity, to finish the will. It was completed and signed on the 26th April 1913, and it was impressive in its specific detail.

The list of people named, and the bequests, were illuminating, and help to build a picture of her life and her experiences. To Miss Rhoda Bethell she gave her *gold watch with black figures and chain, the Indian Paper Bible in my possession, and any horse, dog or cat I may possess at the time of my death*. Rhoda lived in London at the time of the will, and Mary Lily had met her when they were both at the Grey Ladies home in Blackheath. The mention of sundry horses, cats and dogs reveals Lily's great love for animals, and the fact that they are not named would suggest that she had a few and that she intended continuing to do so. Mary and Rhoda spent a great deal of time together at Grey Lodge, and at Roseangle, the cottage in Gauldry. They would also share some holidays together, and Rhoda fondly remembered the hill walks and the alpine flowers, and her joy that Lily could name them, every one. No doubt Lily would have had similar recollections as she put pen to will.

In the case of Meta Peterson, Lily was particularly generous in her bequest. Meta had lived in the same street, Airlie Place, when both girls were readying themselves for their careers at University College. Meta sat in the same classrooms as Lily, and they took year about in winning academic prizes. Meta was there in the best of times, and in the saddest of times, always ready with a word or a deed. Meta was a very special friend to

Mary, and Mary spent a lot of time with Meta's family. They would go off on annual holidays to Italy, sharing long rail journeys in each other's glorious company, and Meta's mother would go along too. Meta's brother had been the first Principal at Dundee, and when he had moved on to a new challenge at McGill University in Montreal, Mary Lily would have said goodbye to him with the same sense of brotherly love, albeit tinged by a little awe, as did his own sisters. Mary Lily and Meta knew each other and each other's families very well, and when the time came to write her will Lily must have sensed her head spinning with memories; a mind filled with recollections of joyous times, tempered by the deep sadness of knowing these things would be no more. She gave Meta one job to do in the will: she specified that Meta should help the Trustees, if necessary, in assisting with the expeditious handing over of her bequests.

The exact wording of the will, insofar as it favoured Meta Peterson, was as follows:

> *To the said Margaret Grace Peterson the whole of my body clothes and wearing apparel and all articles of jewellery belonging to me excepting the foresaid Watch and Chain and any other articles which may be specially bequeathed by me in codicil hereto.*

In leaving these items to Meta, Lily was giving away her most personal possessions to her closest friend, something of which Meta would have been very aware and deeply appreciative.

Meta was also given Villa Venusta, the house in Alassio in Italy where Lily would have remembered many happy holidays, along with all of the furniture, and other goods in both the Villa and Grey Lodge in Dundee that had not been specified to other benficiaries. Meta's sister, Gulielma, was left a bureau and six books of her choosing. Gulielma was much younger than Mary Lily, but would have known her through Lily's very close connection to the family. Gulielma would be the one to register Mary Lily Walker's death. Gulielma resided in Edinburgh, and may well have been summoned on the weekend of Mary Lily's death to join all those loving friends who had gathered at Grey Lodge.

Mary Muirhead Paterson was one of the Trustees of Lily's will, but she was also a beneficiary. Mary Lily considered her a good friend and admired her tireless and important work as an Inspector of Factories. She was left dinner sets and cutlery, and also a particular writing bureau from the drawing room at Grey Lodge. Another Trustee, Alexander Mackay, was left the large, gilt mirror that had hung in the drawing room at Grey Lodge, and also a collection of Charles Booth's Works on London. Booth was a social reformer looking at working class life in London, and his books included works on poverty. Booth's work in social statistics was recognised by the Royal Statistical Society, which bestowed upon him the first Guy Medal, plated in gold, in 1882. His works, if not directly influencing the DSU Report of Mary Lily and Mona Wilson, would no doubt have informed how well statistics might be used. Miss Harriet Menmuir, who was employed by the DSU and had been superintendent at the Nursing Mothers' restaurants, was another to whom Lily showed her appreciation and friendship. She left her a special work-table from Grey Lodge – possibly one from the very restaurant where so much good was done.

To John Sandeman Allen, her Trustee, and one of her few remaining relatives, she left some silver table articles that were marked with either 'A' or 'OA'. These might have belonged to her own mother and the 'A' may well have stood for Allen and 'OA' for Oswald Allen. He was also given a picture of Hackfall, a beautiful location with a sadly decayed old building in

Grewelthorpe, North Yorkshire. This was probably a painting by Albert Kinsley, and may well have originally been bought in October 1877 at 'A Fete for the benefit of the Grewelthorpe Benefice Augmentation Fund' which was held near the Banqueting Hall in Hackfall. Lily's Uncle James Allen was certainly noted as being at this event, and it might be that he, or his sisters, bought it there. John Sandeman Allen's two daughters, Catherine and Frances Amy, were financially provided for in the will, each receiving an annual sum that would increase as time elapsed. There is no way of knowing whether Mary Lily had attended the baptism of either or both of these children, though the fact that their father was chosen and named as Trustee would seem to indicate that she was close to their family, and having no remaining immediate members of the Walker family left, those left in the Allen family would be precious to her.

Travelling to and from the north west of England would certainly not have troubled Lily, and so she may well have been at the baptisms. She was a well-travelled woman who made frequent visits to her Uncle James and her aunts in Kendal. Many letters from Lily, especially to D'Arcy Thomson, are letter-headed with the address, Bank Top, Kendal. This was the home of James Allen where she would have been a most welcome guest. Some of these trips, in the early years, would have been with her mother. The journey south, with the train travelling through mile upon mile of empty scenery broken only by the occasional farm and the dots of hill sheep, must have had them thinking back to the Dundee they had left, where the contrast could hardly have been starker. Mary Lily was also a frequent visitor to London, whether for business or reunions with past colleagues and friends. She also enjoyed the train journey to the far climes of Italy's north Mediterranean coast. Alassio became a highly popular tourist location towards the end of the nineteenth century, and was famed for its beaches and beautiful coastline, and also for its array of walks through stunning countryside into the hills behind. Mary Lily, in the company of Meta, Rhoda, and sometimes with others, would have strolled these hills, and would have been as taken by the flowers and plants as she would have been with the scenery. Her knowledge of botany, honed as it was under the tutelage of geniuses like Geddes and Wentworth Thompson, would have flooded back in these hill walks. The railway connected London to Genoa in 1872, via Alassio. The town had a British Club and a fortnightly newspaper printed in English (the unimaginatively named *Alassio News*). With this idyllic setting, and at times like these, Dundee, the Social Union, and the poverty, overcrowding and deprivation in the town may have been pushed to the back of her mind. But it was never out of her mind.[194]

Alassio would have seemed as far removed from Dundee as it is possible to be and the comfort of Villa Venusta might have served to heighten the sheer enormity of her task in her hometown. She had considered Dundee's problems and realised that many of them stemmed from the greed and apathy of the wealthy elite who owned the mills and factories. Lily knew they had no compunction about lowering wages drastically when it suited, and employing married women and children, knowing well enough how this impacted on the social welfare of the town. She also knew that the council in Dundee, if not populated by the mill-owners themselves, was populated by some of their lackeys. These people blamed the poorest inhabitants for being authors of their own distress and destitution, blaming domestic mismanagement and endemic drunkenness for the misery. Lily knew well where the root of the problem lay, but she also knew that addressing the cause head-on was difficult for her. The very families that she saw as perpetrating the intolerable hardships were the families that she knew, and her mother and father and sisters had known and worked with in all sorts of charitable committees.

These were the people who provided parks in the town, and buildings, and who had, through their businesses, made Dundee a player in global markets.[195] They hardly needed her to jolt them into better wages and conditions for workers, for these elite had deserted the centre of town, moving to the east of the town towards Broughty Ferry, or west to the far reaches of the Perth Road area, or even south into Fife, to escape the sight of men and women in rags and bow-legged children with bare feet in all weathers. Neither would she need to show them the unbelievable level of overcrowding in houses, for they were all too aware that they sucked more and more people, through their expansionist ideals, into the mills and factories of Dundee where new housing was little more than a pipe-dream.[196] Least of all she would have to tell them of the smells and noises of this hometown of theirs: smells of untreated waste; sweat from bodies with difficult access to fresh drinking water, far less bathing water; and noises of street-digging, and of looms clattering and the ear-splitting whirring of machinery. They would have heard even less the crying of cold and starving children, the sobbing of women driven to the edge of despair, and the low moans of the sick and dying, not from the distance of their out-of-town homes, not from the remoteness of their manicured gardens.[197] Mary Lily recognised the essential need for holidays, for herself and others, away from the daily and constant sights and struggles. Coming back refreshed, and with new ideas dreamt up in the dislocation of a holiday, was a far more productive way of approaching matters, and a necessary rest from the fray.[198]

She also had the cottage in the Fife village of Gauldry, where she would try to spend time often. Roseangle: an apt name for the place, a name which brought to her mind *an easy image of fragrant flowers*, but it also shared its name with the Dundee street where Lily scuffed along to school in those days which must have seemed such a long time ago as she sat penning her will. Trips to the Gauldry meant a train ride; a fascinating if short trip across the new bridge over the Tay.[199] Below the new bridge, like decaying teeth, the bared stumps of the old bridge, slightly out of alignment with the new structure, jutted out of the river in a constant reminder of the so recent *'disaster'*, and as a constant line of gravestones to those souls who were lost on that fateful evening.

Lily's train trip took little more than five minutes. Construction of the new bridge had been started in 1883, and it opened to traffic on the 20th June 1887. There was no ceremony, no visits from foreign dignitaries, and there was just a muted sense of achievement in the town. This new *'longest metal structure in the world'* crossed a span that was *'too deep in the emotional heart and too recent to acclaim'*.[200] At Wormit, Lily would alight. Waiting very patiently for her would be the horse and pony-carriage that would take her up the two-mile long road to Roseangle. The beloved little horse was named Donald.[201] As she left the little station, she would cast her eye over the two-mile stretch of water to Dundee, sitting like a lovable grey dog at the foot of the Law, the hill that loomed over the city.

After passing the row of pretty houses leading out of Wormit, the trap would make a right-turn and dip before steadily rising and twisting towards their destination. Donald would need no urging; he knew this road, and his passenger, exceedingly well. Halfway there the sign for Peace Hill Farm would make Lily smile: the name would be symbolic to her. At the top of the rise, just before the Gauldry came into view, they would almost certainly stop at their viewing point.[202] From here, Dundee, wearing the river for a scarf, would be very clear, and so would the billowing smoke from its factory chimneys. Common wisdom of the time declared there were 146. Who could scarce believe it? Then again, who would want to count the number of these textile *'palaces'* and infernal foundries?[203]

Mary Paterson recalled being invited to weekends in the retreat of Lily's, and she remembered the *'cracks'* with Lily *'in the firelight of the upper room with the lights of Dundee dancing and flickering across the Tay'*. She also remembered that Rhoda Bethell was a very frequent guest in the Gauldry cottage. Lily and Rhoda were great companions and went far beyond Fife on their travels together. One trip, in 1910, to the Oberammergau Passion Play held every ten years, meant a week's unforgettable holidaying and walking in the hills of the Austrian Tyrol where Lily's knowledge of botany allowed her to name every one of the dear alpine flowers.[204]

Mrs Brown, *'lovely dutiful Mrs Brown'*, would be ready at Roseangle, with tea brewing and far too many freshly baked goods as ever. She would smile and shake her head as she watched Lily struggle in with all manner of things brought from Dundee: books, furniture and even a dog and cat.[205] The sense of getting away would start for Mary Lily as soon as she alighted from the Edinburgh train, and it would be nourished in many ways once the cottage was entered. In Lily's will there is no mention of Mrs Brown, and while her fate is not known, it can only be adduced that Mrs Brown predeceased her employer. Her caretaker, Alexander Melville, was a beneficiary in the will, where he was bequeathed £50. On his inclusion in the will Lily's thoughts must have settled for a while on Roseangle, and the many times she took friends across to enjoy the simple, wholesome and abundant delights of a place so close to Dundee yet so far away. As one of the beneficiaries, Alexander Melville had the distinction of being, apart from the Trustees, the only male mentioned by name. This is a very clear indicator that Lily's life was proliferated by female colleagues and companions. One male, however, did have a constant and regular place in Lily's work and life, and had done for thirty years. That was, of course, her Trustee, Professor D'Arcy Wentworth Thompson.

As has been mentioned earlier, his academic and social work connections to Lily meant that he was very regularly in her company. She was very fortunate to have such a lecturer and teacher, because, by any measure, he was an authority in his academic field. Born in Edinburgh in May 1860, D'Arcy was barely three years older than his special student. Such little age difference would have impacted on their attitudes towards each other. He was a precocious child in terms of intellectual ability, and his progression into academia was assured from a very early age, given that his father was a classicist and academic whose book, *Daydreams of a Schoolmaster*, published in 1864, revealed his enlightened views on education and his disdain for corporal punishment. The offer of a Professorship in Greek in Queens College, Galway, meant that he rarely saw his son, our D'Arcy, who was left to be brought up by his mother's parents, and especially by his Aunt Pam.[206]

D'Arcy grew to love the classics, inspired by his father's studies, but it would be in science that he would excel. An early interest was kindled by his paternal grandfather, and this was stoked and shaped by a teacher, Buckham Hugh Hossack, a man as passionate about natural history as his young pupil. D'Arcy's schoolboy peers would remark on his ability to stand up and speak on virtually any subject. At Edinburgh Academy, the school his father had taught at before moving to Galway, D'Arcy was called "Daftie", or "Daft Thompson", because he was not very like the other boys there. He was too occupied in his own ideas, or engrossed in some book to play with the other fellows. One of them remarked: *'He's a queer fellow – there was always something about him we couldn't understand'*. In his class were three fellow pupils, John Scott Haldane, Diarmid Noel Paton and William Abbot Herdman, who would all go on to join him as Fellows of the Royal Society of Edinburgh.[207]

D'Arcy went to Edinburgh University in 1878 before moving to take up a degree in Natural Science at Trinity College, Cambridge. He had hoped to gain a Fellowship there, but to no avail. He was successful, however (though he feared he would not be), when he applied to University College, Dundee. He took up his post in January 1885 and offered his inaugural lecture on the 25th January (coincidentally, Burns' Day), the same year. In this speech he delivered the following words: *'There can be only one truth in the fullness of knowledge, and he who works humbly and sincerely to let in light, works not for himself but for all men'.* These were wonderful words that would sum up the work not just of himself but also of Mary Lily Walker.[208]

Thompson's classes were popular, a tribute to both his academic brilliance and his teaching methods, but this popularity led to problems. Very soon he was complaining about the severe shortage of space in which to teach science, causing him to remonstrate that *'My laboratory is barely sufficient to hold three students and my Laboratory Assistant; I have now nearly sixty who desire and ought to avail themselves of it'.* Mary Lily Walker was one of his early students, and he would write of her later through his memory:

> *Mary Lily Walker was a student of mine shortly after I came to Dundee; a young woman like many another, of the simplest, homeliest upbringing, of scanty opportunities, devoted to an invalid mother.*[209]

The longer Lily attended University College, the more she and D'Arcy got to know each other, but it was in the DSU that they would become colleagues, and the relationship began to become one of equals. It was at this time, and regularly right up to Lily's death, that they began to send each other letters. There was nothing unusual about this; writing letters was very much a common practice and the only way to communicate in these days before the telephone was available. Postal Directories had page after page of information on postal services and postal charges, and virtually every country in the British Empire, and very many more besides, had its own listing with its own rate of postage.[210]

As the years passed, the letters between the two became less formal and began to cover more of their everyday experiences. This letter, written on 10th May 1889, shows the familiarity that began to populate their messages:

My dear Miss Lily,

I sent you yesterday a proof, so today Aleck will despatch the paper.

You will see that the proof is a little too Dark, but that will perhaps improve in the outlines, instead of being objectionable are scarcely marked enough.

I came back on Monday, most reluctantly. On Saturday I had a magnificent time at Leopardstown races, nr. Dublin; & lost my money cheerfully.

I am sending you on a post card!

A grieg; Monsieur l'assumee de ma haute considération!

D'arcy W, Thompson[211]

This letter was sent on letter-headed paper from University College, Dundee, and was addressed to Mary Lily at the Grange Hotel, Grange-over-Sands, Lancashire, where presumably she was having some time to herself after the death of her mother a few months before. An earlier letter, also sent to Lily at the Grange Hotel, this time on the 30th March, is similarly seen to contain a mixture of work-associated and personal items:

My dear Miss Lily,

I am still idling utterly. I neither read, write, nor collect: but only eat, drink, & walk about leisurely.

Old Parker has sent us his Tarsipes paper – to Dundee: but it has not yet been forwarded....

I hear a case of specimens from Germany, ordered two years ago, & forgotten, is on its way to Dundee.

I have found some papers by Krause in the Mt. Monatschift of Anatruria wh. have a strong parental likeness to Conar Ewart's on the Eleckin Organ

I am building many castles in the air for research & other work. I have a strong idea we shd. start on a big Text-book of Mammalia – or even Vertebrate-Anatomy. There's no doubt we must stand or fall by Vertebrates. There are too many people working at Invertebrates who know more about them than we do...

I am going out to try & buy a present for Weismann's daughter, who is about to marry Parker's son.

But Galway is not much of a place for shopping.
No news from London yet

Ever yours truly
D'arcy W. Thompson[212]

The familiarity of this letter, sent from Galway, is less evident than the previous one, and it may be that coming so soon after her mother's death, D'Arcy was trying to keep Lily abreast of happenings in his life and at Dundee, simply to make her feel included in events. Lily went south to her uncle's house after her mother's funeral, but must have decided to take time in Grange-over-Sands. She evidently wrote to D'Arcy to tell him of her decision to do this.

A letter from D'Arcy Thomson, posted in Galway on 1st April 1889, thanks Lily for the letter she sent from the Grange Hotel, confirming that the pair are writing to each other quite regularly. A personal card, written by D'Arcy on

25th December 1889, is addressed to Mary Lily at Bank Top, Kendal, revealing that she had returned to the house of her uncle for Christmas.[213]

Another letter, this time dated 15th May of the same year, was sent to Lily at the Grange Hotel, from University College with the following lines in the text:

> *On Friday afternoon, on reaching home. I found on my mantel-piece a card left by Miss Walker, 8 Windsor St. She had been very anxious to see me, & promised to return to day at 11 o' clock.*
>
> *I was in a terrible fright, but I pushed myself up & went to call.*
>
> *It turned out that she only wanted to read yr. scientific works! These I sent her saying she might keep them, but they were returned today, in good condition.*

The Miss Walker in the letter is Lily's half-sister, Anna Louisa, who evidently knew D'Arcy well enough to leave a card at his home. No doubt the funeral of Mary Anne would have been something which both had attended, and it is clear that he had become a familiar figure to all the Walker family.

On 28th June, again in 1889, D'Arcy sent a letter to Lily from the University Club in Edinburgh, an extract from which read:

> *The Petersons asked me to join their picnic tomorrow; but I have had enough of picnics. I supped with the Gourlays – Wednesday & made a great mess of the drawing room carpet, with a conjuring trick wh. Succeeded imperfectly.*
>
> *Yesterday I gave away the medals to the girls of Mr Kerr's school, in Grays' rooms. I made a little speech, & put the ribbons round their necks & under their hair most beautifully.*[214]

The mention of picnics reveals the sort of social gatherings that were common amongst the middle classes in Dundee, where invitations were handed out and party-pieces performed, though in the case of D'Arcy, his conjuring tricks did not match his scientific prowess. Also mentioned is the fact that D'Arcy had been asked to present prizes to pupils from a local school, which shows the close connection between University College and Dundee's schools. The prize-giving was held in Gray's Rooms, across the road from the College, and in the days before they concentrated on funeral directing. The letter was sent to *Miss M.L.Walker, c/o D Hildesheim, Bayond, Lyndhurst Gardens, Hampstead, N.W. London.* Lily's extended stay in Grange-over-Sands had ended, and she was staying with friends in London; the Hildesheims. Both Miss Olga Hildesheim and Miss Evelyn Hildesheim would be beneficiaries in Lily's will, each receiving £100.[215]

A letter sent one month later, on 29th July 1889, finds Lily back in Dundee, and staying at 17 Airlie Place, which may well have been the home of a friend. D'Arcy wrote it in Dublin, and speaks about recent stays in Liverpool, which he liked, and Manchester, which he didn't. He mentions in this letter that he intends heading off to Galway for a month. The mileage being run up by D'Arcy and by Lily during this year is prodigious, and displays the massive difference to social mobility that the railway system brought to Britain and the continent. This theme is continued in a letter of 15th December 1889. Lily is still residing at Airlie Place, presumably readying herself for her Christmas trip to the Allens in Kendal, when this message is sent by D'Arcy from Freiburg in Germany:

My dear Miss Lily,

It will add the enjoyment of the half bottle of Tischwein which I am at this moment engaged in consuming, if I meanwhile write you a short account of my doings.

I am on my way to Berne, to see my unfortunate uncle, Arthur Gamgee, who is unhappily Geistkraank. or, not to put too fine appoint upon it, as mad as a March Hare. I rather shrink from the visit, & am dallying on the way.

Yesterday I came here from Bâla, where I spent two days, chiefly with Professor Rŭtimeyer; the latter is a very celebrated palaeontologist. He entertained me on the highest scale of Teutonic hospitality, with cigars, beer & several hours of extremely interesting conversation. As it came near dinner-time he begged me to return next morning at 8 o'clock!

His collections are superb. I communicated to him my opinion concerning Cope's genus Phenacodus; it co-incided so completely with his own that he embraced me!

Prof. Kollmann, the anatomist in Bâla, is also an excellent man. He gave me a tadpole as big as a frog. He enquired kindly after Aleck, from whom I (imagine that he) had brought some casts of brains a year ago.

He has in his private laboratory a girl who cuts sections, draws & transcribes. She adds to her other excellent qualities that of being deaf & Dumb![216]

This shows D'Arcy's sense of humour, as well as his predilections for the "finer" things of life. Two more letters, both sent from D'Arcy to Lily in August of that year are also revelatory in terms of their relationship. The first, sent from the Saville Club in London where he was a member, begins,

My dear Miss Lily,

I am very sorry about the eyes. You must wrap yourself up in cotton wool & take great care of yourself, & go to Switzerland by hook or by crook....

Tomorrow I may go to Paris – But I'd just as soon stay at home.

Yours ever sincerely
D'arcy W. Thompson[217]

This letter is dated 3rd August, and indicates that Lily has written to him mentioning an eye problem, and that she is considering a trip to Switzerland. A second letter, dated only eight days later, sent from the Hotel Meurice, in Rue de Rivoli, Paris, begins with a mild rebuke to Lily:

My Dear Miss Lily,

You are again maintaining a complete but most unacceptable silence. I have no news of any kind from you, nor even from Aleck ...

I hope to hear from you at the Savile. How about the eyes.

Yours ever D'arcy W. Thompson[218]

This complaint to Lily, after a passage of just eight days, indicates how often the pair must have stayed in touch and the sorts of places and events that they shared details about. It also reveals that there must have been another letter sent by D'Arcy between these two; one that would have revealed his address in Paris. Both letters were addressed to Airlie Place, Dundee, and they stand testimony to the wonderful postal system of the time.

These letters, with their trifling details and their highly personal style for letters of the age, reveal a relationship that far transcended a tutor-student acquaintance. The proximity of academics and students in Dundee's University College was necessarily close because of the confined space in the early days, particularly so in the laboratory of D'Arcy Wentworth Thomson, but it is probable that the involvement which both had in the Dundee Social Union brought them to becoming very good friends. There would be scarcely a thing happening in the lives of either that the other wouldn't know about. In July of 1893, Lily joined a Women's University Settlement in Southwark, London, for a period. D'Arcy knew exactly what these settlements were set up to do, having been very interested in the first such settlement which was opened in London at Toynbee Hall. He would have told Lily about this and encouraged her participation as he felt sympathy for her *'knowing nothing of the world'*.

D'Arcy was a large and imposing figure; his picture in the Royal Society of Edinburgh attests to this.[219] When he first arrived in Dundee he was prone to illness and forever catching cold, had flu or regular bouts of bronchitis and pleurisy. At one time in his second winter in Dundee, he was so ill that he went to stay with his Aunt Pam in Alva Street in Edinburgh for two months. His daughter, Ruth, recalled in a biography, *'It was during this time that he grew his beard; it was as red as his hair, and he was inordinately proud of it'.* This corresponds with the opinion of Agnes Allen (1886–1981) who remembered D'Arcy as being *'Tall, well-built, a head like a lion with a big red beard and a shock of red hair'.*

Modern day commentator, Dr Suzanne Zeedyk, an Honorary Fellow in Developmental Psychology at the University of Dundee, takes an interesting view of the relationship with the words:

> *It gives us a sense of that playful self-impressed quality that Mary Lily Walker teased him about. She helped him not to take himself seriously. She grounded him. They balanced each other; his high energy balanced her serious (probably sometimes doleful, at least in her earlier years) energy.*

They did balance each other in many ways. She was as slight and shy as he was gregarious and big.[220] He was demonstrative and happy to have his opinion heard, while she was effectively productive in a more measured and unobtrusive way. He had a playfulness and a slightly raucous sense of humour, whilst Lily, although fondly remembered for her *delightful humour and gaiety at the mother's tea-parties and little entertainments for children at the Grey Lodge*,[221] was much more reserved and selective in her expressions.

But they had so many common traits too; both were intellectually gifted, what little she lacked against his academic brilliance she more than made up for in clear common sense and aptitude. Both had a passion for social reform, and retained this until their deaths, but his interest was as much theoretical as practical whilst Lily got her hands dirty on countless occasions. Their many letters to each other suggest they enjoyed each other's company, and trusted each other implicitly. Both, as evidenced in the teasing words of many letters, had a great affection for each other. But both seem shy when it came to taking the relationship further. Even the pressed flowers he sent her were kept in their envelopes rather than displayed for anyone to see. D'Arcy's bluff and bluster seemed to have been a façade when it came to close personal involvement, and Mary Lily was neither confident enough, nor forward enough, to change that.

D'Arcy Wentworth Thompson married his stepmother's niece, a young Irish girl called Maureen Drury, in July 1901. They had met in Galway in 1900, and again by chance in Connemara. She was of a delicate disposition, asthmatic, and prone to violent headaches, and he apparently fell deeply in love with her, though she would vex him by insisting her sister went with them when he took her out walking. Maureen was very religious, and had a strong sense of loyalty and fairness, but suffered from extreme nervousness. Even in this relationship, D'Arcy went through torment in the few seemingly endless days it took for Maureen to agree to marry him. She was found to have an ophthalmic goitre after the birth of their second child, something that at the time could only be treated by the patient lying in complete inactivity. D'Arcy had clearly known of Maureen's health problems prior to marrying, and he expressed his acceptance of her problems in a letter to Mary Lily after announcing his engagement when he wrote: *'I thank God that my marriage is not, at least in a worldly way, to be a selfish one; but that with the desire for my own happiness there is to be linked the desire to give happiness to one who has very little'.* Whether or not Lily found any comfort in these words is a matter of guesswork. John Sinclair was D'Arcy's best man at the wedding which took place near Bristol.[222] There is no mention of Mary Lily Walker at the wedding.

Mary Lily left D'Arcy an etching of Rembrandt that had hung in the Grey Lodge dining room, old editions of works by Horace and Virgil, and allowed him any other four books of his choosing. Whilst these were of obvious sentimental value, the bequest to D'Arcy was not prolific, as some others were, although Lily went much further in naming his three daughters, Ruth Thompson, Mary Lily Thompson and Barbara Thompson as financial beneficiaries. How Lily felt when she wrote the three children's names in her will, particularly the name of the daughter bearing her own Christian names, is impossible to tell. Maureen always called her second daughter Molly, rather than Mary Lily.[223]

⁞ ⁞

Mary Lily Walker died at Grey Lodge, in her own bed, on the morning of July 1st, 1913, just four days before her fiftieth birthday. At the end of her life, her doctor, Julia F Pringle, attended her. She lived just around the corner, and worked at Dundee Infants Hospital and at Blackscroft Baby Clinic.[224]

The cause of death was given as septicaemia. Her death was registered the very same day by Gulielma Peterson who was recorded as being present in the house at the time of death. Gulielma was the younger sister of Lily's long-time friend, Meta, and was another woman of accomplishment, being Secretary to the Classics Association in Edinburgh (the sole woman on a board of thirty men). Mary Lily was the last of the Walker family; a family which, right up to the last, had been prominent in Dundee's history.

Septicaemia is a form of blood poisoning, and whilst this may have been the final prognostication, it is not a lingering or predictable occurrence. Mary Lily knew she was dying much earlier in that year. Her obsession in writing a will and putting things in order are proof enough that she saw, and felt, her demise coming. But other people, too, picked up on this message. Her friend, Dr Emily Thomson, with whom she had instigated the Dispensary and Clinic for Women in the Hilltown, Dundee (an idea that successfully outgrew its boots until it became the Women's Hospital), remembered a time in Gauldry, quite shortly before her death, when Mary Lily uttered the words: *'I want Dundee to have the Grey Lodge when I go, but only if Dundee will make use of it. It must not be merely a monument to me'.*[225] This desire to have no *'monuments'* epitomised the humility of the woman, and her pragmatism.

Dr Freeland Barbour, who had been a member of the Royal Commission for Housing, remembered being summoned, quite urgently, one day to the Grey Lodge. This, she remembered, was in June 1913, and she recalled:

> *we had a long talk sitting on the lawn in front of its windows. She spoke of the various influences which had led her to find her main life-work in the activities of the Social Union, and went on to say that, though she seemed at the moment*

in good health, she had reason to think that the final call,
when it came, would almost certainly come suddenly ... just
a fortnight later the call came for which she had so well
prepared.[226]

That call meant Mary Lily had died.

Registration of death in Scotland had been mandatory for almost sixty years by the time of Lily's death. But by 1913 there were still instances of deaths not being registered, particularly, and most markedly, in the Highlands and Islands of Scotland. The Dewar Report of 1913 stated that as many as seventy percent of deaths in some parishes (Kilmuir on the Isle of Skye was singled out) failed to be registered. It is thought the number of unregistered deaths in the town and cities was much lower but might still run to around five percent. The cause of death, too, was not always accurate, as doctors would use generic terms to euphemise certain conditions. Septicaemia, according to a recent Cambridge University Paper, was very often the term used in Scotland when particular cancers had been diagnosed. This was not deemed unlawful, and in cases such as suicide or venereal diseases, the cause given saved trauma and stigmatisation for families.

Whether Lily had a cancer or not, she clearly bore whatever ailment she felt she had with composure and stoicism. Mary Paterson said: *'We who knew her and loved her ... were stunned by the blow of her death. For she was taken as in a moment while in a flood of activity'.* Another friend, Denny Oliphant wrote to D'Arcy Thompson saying: *'I saw and had a talk with her on the last Friday ... when she seemed perfectly well'.* Even Dr Emily Thomson found her death *'unexpected'.* Mary Lily Walker's death was un-trumpeted, in the same way she tried to make sure her life had been.

Her funeral was directed by William C Norrie & Son, who operated their undertaking firm from premises at 9–11 Shore Road, Dundee, where they also dealt in antique furniture, and made upholstered goods and cabinets. They had also handled the funerals of Lily's half-sisters, Grace and Eliza. Their telephone number was Dundee195 for those modern enough to be able to call them. The funeral service was held on Thursday 3rd July in St Pauls Cathedral, the church she had attended with her mother and where in later years she had usually attended the 9.00am Sunday service with its traditional liturgy. It was also the church where her adored mother's funeral service had been held twenty-four years previously. Lily's service started at 1.30pm and the coffin and the body of Mary Lily Walker were to be interred in Balgay Cemetery. William C Norrie & Son expressly asked intended mourners to advise them if they would be *'desiring to accompany the cortege'*.[227] Their reason in asking was to inform the authorities because of the likelihood of a long procession. A newspaper photograph, showing the mourners departing St Paul's Cathedral after the service, gave an indication of the crowds who came to pay tribute, and the gleaming top hats and elegant mourning dresses are juxtaposed with the everyday bonnets showing how much of a cross-section of public grief was on display.[228]

The route of the horse-drawn cortege was up the High Street, passing the door at 2 High Street where her father and grandfather had once run their writer's businesses, up to the Nethergate, where her school and her University College premises sat opposite each other, past Airlie Place to the right where Meta and she had become such wonderful friends, then past the house at 152 Perth Road where Mary Lily's life journey had begun. From there it continued west on Perth Road, passing St Peter's Church where Eliza, Anna Louisa and Grace had spent so many Sundays. There is no indication whether it turned right at Sinderins to climb Blackness Avenue, or carried on past the houses at Windsor Terrace where Lily and her mother had spent the first few years after Thomas Walker's death, then up past Western Cemetery where her father and two of her stepsisters lay. It is more likely, given the gradients of the roads up towards Balgay, that Blackness Avenue would have been the option.

The hearse would wait near to the hilly spot, marked by the Celtic Cross, where Mary Lily Walker's remains would be placed beside those of her stepsister Grace, her brother, Arthur Thomas John, and her mother, Mary Anne Allen. This was almost as Lily had thought it would eventually be when her mother was buried apart from her husband, Thomas. The crowds of mourners would have found it difficult to get very near to the lair, but would have been near enough to hear the graveside service and to witness the lowering of her coffin. Amongst the dressed-up crowd might well have been some of the tenants, and the women and children, to whom she had willingly given herself.

ℬ ℭ

There is mourning among a little band of fellow-workers. There is sorrow behind many a door which, in her frequent errands the Grey Lady came. Of a truth, she rests from her labours. She has pleaded the cause of the poor and needy, and her deeds shall be told of for a memorial. Her name will be admired among the honourable women, and rich and poor shall meet together by her grave.

These words, from D'Arcy Wentworth Thompson, appeared in the *Dundee Advertiser* on 2nd July 1913, the day after her death. The suddenness of her death brought a shock to all who knew her, and very soon the realisation of the enormous vacuum she had left hit home. People cried, not just because they had lost

185

such a vital force, but they had lost an irreplaceable champion. A day after the obituary by Thompson was printed the *Dundee Advertiser* included a note of tribute from the Dundee Parish Council, a part of which read:

> *her death had come as a great shock to them all, as they saw her, as it seemed, hale and hearty only a week ago ... Miss Husband said she had been closely associated with Miss Walker not only in connection with the Parish Council but in other directions. Miss Walker and herself were the first women to sit as members of the Council, and they had worked together for the good of Dundee.*

It might also have been noted that Miss Walker was soon to become the only woman member of the Parish Council and that, at every turn, the male members had given her little or no support in her endeavours to work for the good of Dundee.

The Cathedral Church Magazine of St Pauls Cathedral in Dundee, in its August 1913 edition, mentioned a note to communicants sent on 3rd July of that year which stated that

> *the unexpected death of Miss Walker, Grey Lodge, will be received with deep regret by the members of the congregation. She has been one of our faithful members and regular communicants, and she will be especially missed ...We thank God for the example of her devoted life. May she rest in peace.*

The *Dundee Advertiser* ran its own copious obituary on Wednesday 2nd July. As well as paying thanks and tribute to the life of *'one of Dundee's noblest daughters'* the paper gave some detail about her death. It stated she *'was in her usual health until about Friday last, when an obscure and dangerous illness manifested itself. She grew rapidly worse and on Monday her condition was recognised as precarious. She passed away about nine o'clock yesterday morning'.* This article goes on, at some length, to extol the many achievements of Mary Lily, and gives huge emphasis to her almost single-handedly being responsible for the success of Dundee Social Union. The most telling lines though, and the ones above all that might have pleased Lily, were:

> *Among the intellectual and cultured she had many friends, and among the poor and ignorant she had many more. Today the east end, no less than the west end, mourns the death of a lady who, wherever she went, was the shining example of a noble life devoted to a noble and self-sacrificing cause.*

Mona Wilson, the intelligent woman with whom Lily had shared the arduous writing of the DSU's 1905 Report met with her once or twice after its conclusion when they travelled on holidays together. The last time they had done so was in the spring of 1913 when they had enjoyed '*a long tramp in the Tyrol with the flowers at their best, staying at some of the villages which were soon to be wrecked'.* Although Mona would not know it at the time, Mary Lily must have taken that final trip with the friend she had worked with and had grown so much to love with the thought of her impending death in her mind. Mona, a very sophisticated and cultured lady who mixed in high social planes, remarked of Lily:

> *To me her death meant the loss of a companion with whom every interest and enjoyment and joke could be shared.*

The emotional devastation felt by those who had known Lily well was seen in letters immediately after her death. Meta Peterson wrote to D'Arcy Thompson on 5th July 1913, which would have been Lily's fiftieth birthday, about something anomalous in the will, which D'Arcy had noticed.[229]

16 Murrayfield Road   *5th July 1913*
Murrayfield

Dear Mr Thompson

Thank you for writing to me so fully. It is a very unfortunate difficulty that you tell me about in the Will & I am like you quite satisfied that that was not her intention. I hope it may be got over – Anybody can see that there could be no advantage to anyone in such an arrangement – on the contrary the disadvantage is serious.

I did not know anything further than the provision for Miss Irving & myself. Lily told me about that in April. I did not know about the Villa & I hope you will allow me to write to you about that again after a while.

I believe the agent in Alassio is Miss Manlon – I do not know her further address but I think the name would find her. It used to be Mr Walter Congreve, & after him Mr J Congreve: but things were not quite satisfactory under the latter & then it put in Miss Manlon's hands.

On Thursday afternoon I did not feel I could be of any use at the moment & felt very unable to stay longer. But Miss Menmuir promised to let me know if I could help in any way after I had rested & recovered a little from the shock – It has been a terrible week but there's comfort in remembrance.

I am
Yours very sincerely
Meta Peterson

Thursday had been the day of the funeral, and Meta had felt unable to stay for long. Denny Oliphant had not managed to be there at all, because she was fulfilling her promise to look after Madge's children, the same children Lily had loved so much. Denny wrote to D'Arcy, seeing him as the only person she could speak to about her grief, and giving him her thoughts:

...she seems built up with the very dearest and most sacred memories, and which she must remain part of 'til all is past. All her life of devotion and endeavour and achievement are to me a thing apart – a continual source of awe and wonderment. But it is her own self – her great goodness and tenderness and friendship to us in those bitter days ... that make her feel, to us, a piece of ourselves.[230]

Other tributes, other letters poured in. A special meeting of the Dundee Social Union was held and the following lines were selected from their Minute Book: '*Much of her activity was the nature of pioneer work, the fruit of which must come later ... time will prove in great degree the value of this pioneer work*'.

In the same vein, Mary Paterson wrote:

coming generations should learn something of the woman to whose ability and devoted service the City of Dundee owes no small debt. She was a friend, an advisor, and an example of an outstanding influence in many lives ... She gave, ungrudgingly her time and talents, giving unstilted support to every measure designed to reduce poverty, ill-health or overwork, taking often the unorthodox, but never the narrow view.[231]

There was so much unfinished business when Mary Lily Walker passed away, yet her influence and inspiration was such that those around her, and those left on committees that were all the emptier for her absence, all carried on with greater effort. The correspondence and obituaries indicate her kindness and goodness. They were to become part of the legacy left behind by a special woman who, quite simply, gave herself for others.

Denny Oliphant, in a letter D'Arcy, asked the rhetorical question: *'What more, after all, did the saints do?'* [232]

What more indeed?

Chapter 8

Legacy

In his Presidential Address on the occasion of the 'Fiftieth Annual General Meeting of the Grey Lodge Settlement Association' Sir D'Arcy Wentworth Thompson permitted himself the luxury of looking back on some of his most cherished memories. The Hall was hushed, although D'Arcy's stentorian voice had lost little of its power despite his advancing years.

He spoke of ghosts; people who had started the Dundee Social Union all those fifty years earlier. He spoke of the academics; that halcyon group of indecently young professors, incredibly able, who had banded together to examine and combat the dire conditions which too many Dundonians were living in. Ewing, Haldane, Carnelley, Stegall – the names tripped off his tongue, and half-remembered faces suddenly came to mind. Test tubes and policemen, rent-collecting and stenches all came back. Fifty years was a long time and even minds as full and as brilliant as D'Arcy's could be forgiven the odd lapse, but, when it came to remembering the Grey Lady that night, his mind was as crystal clear.

Those early days; he remembered a young student, impossibly shy yet incredibly eager, taking on her education and her life in the same earnest way. Or so it seemed. Once familiarity was found she joined their Dundee Social Union, and her powers turned out to outweigh any, and all, of the others. The dutiful devoted daughter turned her sense of duty and her devotion to another cause once her mother had died. They had missed her when she took herself away to grieve and then again when she trained in London. He remembered the despair she felt when a close friend died of scarlet fever days after giving birth to her third child.

He then recalled the Lady in Grey who returned from the religious settlement in Blackheath. She came back and started the Grey Lodge at her home in Wellington Street – the very place where they were gathered that night. She had been born to be compassionate in the way that few women are, and even fewer men.

Then D'Arcy took his audience for a jaunt through time; a night ride around the filthiest, darkest, dankest tenements in the city. To a place where a nose was a liability and eyes were a great blessing. An abacus would have been handy to count the inhabitants in rooms that were small enough to leave no hiding place, and any fingerless hand could have counted the number of toilets in the block. People lived here and they died here: the women who grew old before their time; the men with sunken, dead-eyed faces; and their children who lived shoeless and hopeless and oft-times sewn into last year's fashion.

To help them you had to know them, and to know them you had to visit them; and again, and again. Mary Lily Walker knew them. *'It is strange how soon we grow accustomed to the sight of misery'*, he said, and maybe he was right... for him, for most people. She would never grow accustomed, dared never to grow accustomed, to the misery.

He offered his audience images of Nursing Mother's Restaurants – a picture of the inside, empty white plates at the ready on spartan tables. "There would have been no pictures without Mary Lily", he may well have reminded them, "and empty plates would stay that way without her". And no Grey Lodge either, without her.

Was she there that night?

Did she watch over her precious Union in her beloved settlement? D'Arcy Thompson obviously thought not, for he spoke of her memory like a long-gone summer.

Then on he went to recent days, to straitened times. He lauded the four wardens who, one after the other since Lily's departure, had graced their role, and he remembered Alexander Mackay: *'never a wiser leader of a truer friend had this House'*. Alexander Mackay, who, too, had given of himself and given of his purse.

And he was back, back to where things started, and to the Grey Lady. To tumultuous applause and reddened eyes he concluded, *'I have not been blessed in my long life with dearer or more honoured friends than Mary Lily Walker and Alexander Mackay'*.

ಐ ಚ

It would be easy to start the idea of legacy, of what Mary Lily Walker's time on this earth left us, by considering the finite things she left and the monies she willed. It would be easy, but it would not be a starting point. The starting point needs to be a state of mind and a sense of history. The state of mind has to be about the art of giving, and the history about how best to give. The first legacy of Mary Lily is learning about how to achieve both.

A right time and a right place has been crucial to anyone who has achieved beyond normal expectations. Mary Lily had Dundee, and nowhere could have needed her more, and she lived in a period of enormous change where giving was considered to be an honourable pursuit, but where "giving of yourself" was a strange concept.

She was given two talents, which were intelligence and compassion, and the fates conspired to guide these gifts where they would. With a younger father and without an invalid mother, things would have been different. Without University College, and with D'Arcy Thompson, they would have been more different still.

Mary Lily picked up ideas in London from the indomitable Octavia Hill: ideas, but not her manner. Though some ideas wilted in Dundee's peculiar patch, other ideas blossomed and adapted themselves in her mind. Without university education she would never have gone, because the extended visit was to a University Settlement. Then later, she went back to London, compelled through emotion and grief, to the Grey Ladies this time, and returned imbued with a deep but personal belief, and with fortitude allied to a sense of organisation.

Grey Lodge emerged from the fruits of those experiences, and won its reputation from Mary Lily's notion of how best to give. Training social workers, those who were keen to learn and to follow that life-path was a key, but so too was reviving the interest of local volunteers. Talks, lectures and leadership from the front went a long way to help, but enthusiasm and a willingness to work so that others might eat – that helped more. All these things were the first legacy Mary Lily Walker gave to Grey Lodge, and they remained as vital and as true as ever through good times and through all times.

Her second legacy was memory; is memory. Immediately after she died, those around her redoubled their efforts, out of respect for her work and love for her. This memory was passed on day by day. Her high standards are the remembered standards. As the years drift by memories of people change and memories are added to, and eventually memories fade except for the edges. Memories of Mary Lily Walker's faded – less so in her settlement Lodge, but there too. It took dusty leaflets of bygone times, written by some who had passed away as Lily had, to occasionally jog long-forgotten treasures.

But standards do not change, and remembered standards do not fade from the mind easily. Without standards nothing lasts, and without the memory of standards, things slip until they can slip no more. In the Grey Lodge it is known, still, that standards were set, and can only be allowed to slip if they are forgotten.

The third legacy she left was caring for children. Not 'childcare' – a modern term that can scare more than it comforts, but caring; caring for children, playing with them and comforting them. The passion that Mary Lily Walker held dearest, and the impetus for every scrap of work she ever did, was caring for children. The first time she set foot in one of those houses (hovels might be a more accurate term) back in 1888, she must have been shocked at the conditions, disturbed by the overcrowding, desperate about the sanitation, but most of all, distraught to see the children.

Poor children would not have been a new sight to her. She lived within yards of the bottom of Step Row, and not much further away was Paton's Lane. Both these Dundee streets had bare-footed ill-clad children aplenty, all in need of a good feed. But things were different when they were inside an overcrowded house, when siblings were huddled against mothers for warmth, and if they were lucky, for love. Caring for children came naturally to Lily, and it ran deeply.

Her time on Dundee Parish Council was not something she relished but something she was prepared to thole in order to work for the welfare of Dundee's poorest, but first and foremost it was for the mothers and their children. Her care for mothers was very real, but it was less for their welfare and more about helping mothers to help children. The Nursing Mother's Restaurant was more of the same. Feeding mothers, so that they might be better equipped to nourish and nurture their children, was a novel idea, brought, like so many very fine things, from Paris. The sight of young faces at peace and untroubled was the pleasure that she enjoyed most, and her awkwardness among those she did not know vanished completely in the company of the children.

The Milk Depots for Children, The Infants' Clinic, the country holidays, the Invalid Children's Hospital, all initiatives designed to better the lot of children; to care for children. She put herself out, chaired and sat on countless committees, hounded the School Board, badgered the town council, appeared at Royal Commissions, influenced national reforms, learned Insurance Acts and gave of herself, all in the quest to care for children, right up to that moment when there was nothing of herself left to give.

This legacy is a shared one; a part stays at the Grey Lodge and the other goes to the Early Years Movement. Mary Lily blamed conditions, rather than parents, for the plight of the children and for the dreadful mortality rate in Scotland. Drinking was the effect and not the cause of this, in her opinion. With a better home environment much could be achieved, and, with a good home environment, children had a much better chance of surviving, even thriving. She was proof of that. Her own childhood had not wanted for emotional or physical sustenance, and she had thrived.

This legacy of early years care has been passed to the Early Years Movement, through the work of Lily and other social reformers since.

Home learning environment in the early years is the largest factor in attainment and achievement at age 10, bigger even than the effect of pre-school and primary school. The Millennium Cohort Study provided evidence of significant inequalities in development at age 3 that can persist throughout people's lives. Supporting parents to provide a stimulating and supportive home environment, particularly in the early years, combined with high quality pre-school and school education is therefore a key element in delivering solidarity and cohesion and improving participation and productivity within the Scottish economy.[233]

Lily wrote, in her seminal Report of 1905, that what happened during pregnancy affected the life, or even ended the life, of a child. The modern Movement declares that *'high-risk behaviour such as substance misuse, smoking and poor diet during pregnancy, and the early years, can have a serious impact on a child's health, development and outcomes'.*[234] Mary Lily's legacy of caring for children goes on today, in Dundee and throughout Scotland. Though the environment may be different, and all have the dignity of shoes, the message has the same honesty and urgency, but fortunately more support.

Caring for children became a watchword at Grey Lodge, and of all the various things that have come and gone since Mary Lily Walker's own presence, the caring for children has remained a constant priority. Clubs for girls were the early emphasis, and that has changed somewhat as culture and social identities have evolved. Through the years when Christian culture promoted Girl Guides and Boys Brigades, the settlement provided a venue and a focus and pack leaders. Better times took away the need to feed, other than to feed the minds of those who attended, and the settlement learned and remembered that the best way to care and to keep attentive minds is to teach them something they want to know.

Mary Lily Walker left her house in the hands of her trustees so that it might be used, through its Settlement House status, *'to provide a focus for social work, and a place of training for ladies engaged in such work'*. The trustees were to evaluate matters after three years to see if things were worth persevering with. Efforts had continued, with Miss Barbour as Superintendent, and well enough for the trustees to convey the Grey Lodge to the permanent keeping off the appointed committee.

Most of the old tenement properties, where the Social Union had started their efforts, were sold to the town after the First World War, and a holiday home for Dundee children was purchased in Blairgowrie. Mary Lily would have approved. Then a training scheme was introduced which brought together Grey Lodge, the DSU and the University. The three institutions closest to the heart of Lily combined to offer students a Social Study Course, where theory was taught in the University, and practical training was given at Grey Lodge. The close co-operation between University and local training school was unique, and this spirit of co-operation and connection, made possible by Mary Lily's trust disposition, and her own life's journey, was the final legacy.

St Margaret's Hostel, immediately to the north of Grey Lodge and only fifty yards distant, was bought in 1920. It had been a Working Girls Home and had been owned by Mrs Alice Mackenzie, the wife of Episcopalian Bishop Mackenzie of Argyll and the Isles at Deengallon, Oban.[235] It would become more and more handy, and used until it eventually became the sole building. Classes began in the 1920s (needlework, cookery, carpentry and gymnastics) providing uses for growing fingers and exercise for legs and minds. The place was alive with tea-parties and picnics, games on Mary Lily's lawn, and happy feet dancing in her corridors. Billiards and bagatelle attracted people, and holes for putting peppered part of the garden. A

Savings Bank for collecting "holiday" money was based in Carnegie Street, in the very building that had been her "milkie school".

The connection to the University continued. D'Arcy Thompson and a number of other professors and staff and students helped with classes or fund-raising bazaars sometimes held in College grounds. Into the 1930s and still the profile was reinforced by the interested visitors, and plays were rehearsed before being acted out in the Little Theatre off Dundee's Victoria Road. The Ministry of Labour rented the building to give classes to unemployed women and men, just as Mary Lily had tried to do through her involvement in the Dundee Distress committee days. The Earl of Airlie came and tried his hand at billiards. Meetings were attended by Lady Provosts and MPs such as Florence Horsburgh. The Prince of Wales came in 1933. His visit rekindled interest in the settlement, and the 400 members became 700 in a short time. He was told all about Mary Lily Walker, all that she had done, and of her legacy. The Prince arranged for the *Illustrated London News* to send an artist, Bryan de Grineau, to record the vital work that the settlement was doing, and so the girls' sewing class and the cookery class in Mary Lily Walker's kitchen were captured forever in print and broadcasted across the entire nation.

Dundee Social Union formally combined names with the settlement, and the "Grey Lodge" became the focus, and the name, that went forward. The settlement became the only one left in Scotland, and although the Second World War could not curb the efforts, diminishing funding could, and the movement of the people out of the city into housing schemes also affected attendances.

Then, in 1948, the last link to the past had gone. Sir D'Arcy Wentworth Thompson died in his bed in St Andrews on the 21st June. He was 88 years of age and had served the Union for sixty years, and for all that time he never lost his interest, nor did the work of the DSU have a diminished place in his enormous heart. He had taken ill shortly after returning from an extended trip to Delhi, where he had talked on care for children.

He was there at the beginning and, as much as anyone, he influenced Mary Lily. With a different wind, he might have married her. He knew all about giving, and how best to give; he knew about memories and remembered, always, the standards she set; he knew about caring for children, their minds and bodies, and he lived for co-operation and connections, particularly with the University and the town. He had been one of her Trustees who had doled the final legacy and remembered, longingly, the one who had asked for his help.

Today the Grey Lodge Settlement continues. Rocky roads have been, and continue to be, crossed. Holiday trips still exist, though further afield, and in different tongues. Clubs still flourish; volunteers still do the unsung work that always happened, and trained staff continue to busy themselves for children and others. Communities meet for sympathy and tea, gossip and important meetings, games, sports, all of which are fostered in the original spirit, if in very different circumstances. The Grey Ladies House is gone, but it was only ever stones, and its proceeds heaped more of Mary Lily's legacy onto her vision. The middle-aged and the elderly of Dundee all know of the Grey Lodge; maybe where they went dancing, or where they watched plays. One, brought up in the Blue Mountains behind the West Port, an area of kind people and unkind conditions, penned this poem about the Mary Lily of whom she had heard:

Twa (in memory of Mary Lily Walker)

Boarn jist a few shoart oors apert,
twa lassies, ain weel-aff, ain puir,
raised in the Megdlen Green an the Burn
in the drone o the bummer's blare.

Fev meenits sprint atween thir hooses bit
it micht've been the erth an the muin,
fir thae kent nuthin o each ither's days
in thir stoory, east-coast toon.

Ain hid a preevileged toffee nose
the ither wis in povertie,
bit education wid show the twa
thir wir ither wyes ti be.

Baith learned at skail how ti read an write
an French an Latin tae,
they learned aboot injustice in thir ain hame toon
an whit social class kid dae.

It kid bear yi up, it kid peen yi doon
it kid mak yir life or spile it;
it kid mak things easy or mak them hard
yi kid love life, or revile it.

They baith stuck in an made thir wye,
the weel-aff lass an the puir ain,
they learned aboot how the ither half lived,
how it mettered how ithers wir farin'.

The lassie fae the Megdlen Green
wid turn tae philanthropie
wid shift the world fir threidbare bairns
fae grindin' povertie.

Shid show mithers how tae keep a hoose
an, tho they wir doon-at-heel,
mak the best o whit they hid
ti keep thir bairnies weel.

The lassie fae the Scourin' Burn
fund a joab at a local skail,
teachin' many a hapless sowl
thit they didna hiv tae fail.

They baith wir a credit in thir different wyes
twa lassies fae Dundee,
spent aa thir days cheengin' ithers' lives
findin' better wyes tae be.

Fran Baillie 2013

ဆ   ော

Years passed, and Mary Lily's name was scarcely mentioned
as time went on. Despite all of her efforts and sacrifices, she
undeservedly became a woman forgotten in time. It took the
work of a Canadian lady (herself a prize-winning academic)
to rekindle vital but almost-forgotten memories, and give new
life to the extraordinary life and determination of one amazing
woman.

Myra Baillie, now sadly deceased, brought Mary Lily
Walker back to the public; this book was written to
add something to that memory that should be forever
in our minds. As Mary Anne Radmacher once said:
'*Courage doesn't always roar. Sometimes courage is the quiet
voice at the end of the day saying "I will try again tomorrow"*'.

Mary Lily Walker was this quiet voice. Despite adversity, both
in the streets around her and in her own private world, Mary
Lily never gave up. Though quiet, gentle and shy in nature, she

refused to ignore the suffering around her and made it her life's work to aid those less fortunate than herself.

Thanks to this book, Mary Lily has refused to fade into the background. Through Myra's hard work to bring Mary Lily's life finally to the spotlight, she can be appreciated and admired as she should be.

1st July 2013 is the 100th anniversary of the death of Miss Mary Lily Walker of Dundee.

Endnotes

Chapter 1

1 Ed. A W Paton & A H Millar, *British Association 1912 Dundee Handbook*

2 *Dundee Postal Directory 1859–60*

3 *Dundee Courier* 6th July 1863

4 *The Herald July* 7th 1863

5 *Lloyd's Weekly Newspaper* (London, England), Sunday, July 5, 1863; Issue 1076

6 *The Dundee Courier & Argus* Thursday, July 10, 1863

7 Marriage Registration accessed at *Find My Past*

8 John Stewart, 'Sickness & Health', in Edited by Lynn Abrams and Callum Brown, *A History of Everyday Life in Twentieth-Century Scotland* (Edinburgh University Press 2010)

9 Death certificate registration document

10 Moore Brown and Dixon LLP, Tewkesbury

11 Early Notification of Birth Act 1907

12 Thomas Walker's Will

13 *Dundee Postal Directory 1864–65*

14 *Dundee Postal Directory 1864–65*

15 C A Whatley, D B. Swinfen, A M Smith, *The Life and Times of Dundee* (John Donald, Edinburgh 1993)

16 ibid

17 ibid

18 Ed. A W Paton & A H Millar, *British Association 1912 Dundee Handbook*

19 ibid

20 *Dundee Postal Directory 1864–65*

21 Ed. A W Paton & A H Millar, *British Association 1912 Dundee Handbook*

22 Census Records 1871

23 Census Records 1871

24 *The Dundee Courier & Argus* (Dundee, Scotland), Thursday, October 08, 1863; Issue 3171

25 1867 British Association Report

26 M Shafe, *University Education in Dundee 1881–1981: A Pictorial History*

27 *1867 British Association for the Advancement of Science Report*

28 ibid

29 ibid

30 C A Whatley, D B. Swinfen, A M Smith, *The Life and Times of Dundee* (John Donald, Edinburgh 1993)

31 Ed. J Tomlinson & C A Whatley, *Jute No More* (Dundee University Press 2011)

32 Chas McKean, 'Beautifying and Improving the City: The Pursuit of Momumental Dundee during the Twentieth Century', Ed. J Tomlinson & C A Whatley, *Jute No More* (Dundee University Press 2011)

33 C A Whatley, D B. Swinfen, A M Smith, *The Life and Times of Dundee* (John Donald, Edinburgh 1993)

34 Walter E Houghton, *The Victorian Frame of Mind* (Yale University Press 1957)

35 *Dundee Postal Directories 1860–70*

36 *Dundee Postal Directory 1847–48*

37 From research by Peter Kinnear from handbooks & directories

38 C A Whatley, D B. Swinfen, A M Smith, *The Life and Times of Dundee* (John Donald, Edinburgh 1993)

39 ibid

40 Rob Duck, 'Physical Development of the Tay Estuary' in Ed. J Tomlinson & C A Whatley, *Jute No More* (Dundee University Press 2011)

41 C A Whatley, D B. Swinfen, A M Smith, *The Life and Times of Dundee* (John Donald, Edinburgh 1993)

42 *Dundee Postal Directories 1860–70*

43 ibid

44 Ed. A W Paton & A H Millar, *British Association 1912 Dundee Handbook*

45 ibid

Chapter 2

46 http://www.cumbriacountyhistory.org.uk/township/kirkby-lonsdale

47 ibid

48 ibid

49 ibid

50 Information courtesy of David Dobson, Historian

51 James Cant – St Andrews Parish Church Dundee

52 http://www.cumbriacountyhistory.org.uk/township/kirkby-lonsdale

53 Peter Kinnear research

54 Chas McKean, 'Beautifying and Improving the City: The Pursuit of Momumental Dundee during the Twentieth Century', Ed. J Tomlinson & C A Whatley, *Jute No More* (Dundee University Press 2011)

Chapter 3

55 *Dundee Postal Directories 1872–76*

56 *Then and Now – A History*

57 Chas McKean, 'Beautifying and Improving the City: The Pursuit of Momumental Dundee during the Twentieth Century', Ed. J Tomlinson & C A Whatley, *Jute No More* (Dundee University Press 2011)

58 ibid

59 *Dundee Postal Directories 1872–76*

60 *Courier & Argus* 7471 3rd July 1877

61 *Courier & Argus* 7474 6th July 1877

62 *Courier & Argus* 7496 3rd August 1877

63 Ed. A W Paton & A H Millar, *British Association 1912 Dundee Handbook*

64 C A Whatley, D B. Swinfen, A M Smith, *The Life and Times of Dundee* (John Donald, Edinburgh 1993) p107

65 Registration of Death document

66 *1867 British Association Report*

67 M Shafe, *University Education in Dundee 1881–1981: A Pictorial History*

68 M Shafe, *University Education in Dundee 1881–1981: A Pictorial History*

69 ibid

70 *Fifty Years Ago and Now* pp8–9

Chapter 4

71 ibid

72 ibid

73 *Fifty Years Ago and Now* p10

74 *Fifty Years Ago and Now* p4

75 ibid

76 *Fifty Years Ago and Now* pp8–9

77 Myra Baillie – Open Dissertation, *Mary Lily Walker of Dundee*

78 Emma Wainwright *Constructing gendered workplace 'types': The weaver-millworker distinction in Dundee's jute industry c.1880–1910* (Routledge 2010)

79 Ed. A W Paton & A H Millar, *British Association 1912 Dundee Handbook*

80 Myra Baillie – Open Dissertation, *Mary Lily Walker of Dundee*

81 Emma Wainwright *Constructing gendered workplace 'types': The weaver-millworker distinction in Dundee's jute industry c.1880–1910* (Routledge 2010)

82 Myra Baillie – Open Dissertation, *Mary Lily Walker of Dundee*

83 Episcopacy in Dundee

84 Ed. A W Paton & A H Millar, *British Association 1912 Dundee Handbook*

85 Burials & Cremations, Dundee library

86 Myra Baillie – Open Dissertation, *Mary Lily Walker of Dundee*

87 Myra Baillie – Open Dissertation, *Mary Lily Walker of Dundee*

88 Octavia Hill – Letter to Fellow Workers 1890 p1

89 *Fifty Years Ago and Now* pp10–11

90 Charles Boot, *Treatise on Poverty*

91 Myra Baillie – Open Dissertation, *Mary Lily Walker of Dundee*

92 ibid

93 DWT Papers 44660 University of St Andrews, Special Collection

94 DWT Papers 44673 University of St Andrews, Special Collection

95 *Fifty Years Ago and Now* p10

96 Chas McKean, 'Beautifying and Improving the City: The Pursuit of Momumental Dundee during the Twentieth Century', Ed. J Tomlinson & C A Whatley, *Jute No More* (Dundee University Press 2011)

97 Mary M Paterson, *Some Memories – Mary Lily Walker of Dundee* p17

98 *Dundee Courier & Argus*, February 4th 1902

99 (reminiscences of Sturge Moore sent to Marie Sturge Moore, Sturge Moore MSS, 25/126B)

100 Mary M Paterson, *Some Memories – Mary Lily Walker of Dundee* p17

101 *Oxford Dictionary of Biographies* (Oxford 2013)

102 1905 DSU Report

103 Overlaying was the term used when a child died because its mother of father had lain on top of it in sleep

104 Myra Baillie – Open Dissertation, *Mary Lily Walker of Dundee*

105 *Dundee Courier* 22nd September 1905

106 Myra Baillie – Open Dissertation, *Mary Lily Walker of Dundee*

107 *The Times*, 2nd March 1907

108 *Working Among Women* – Dundee Handbook

109 *Fifty Years Ago and Now* pp10–11

110 Myra Baillie – Open Dissertation, *Mary Lily Walker of Dundee*

111 *Working Among Women* – Dundee Handbook

Chapter 5

112 Mary M Paterson, *Some Memories – Mary Lily Walker of Dundee*

113 Mary M Paterson, *Some Memories – Mary Lily Walker of Dundee* p10

114 Matthew Jarron & Cathy Caudwell, *D'Arcy Thomson and his Zoology Museum in Dundee* (UoD Museum Services 2010)

115 Ed. D'Arcy W Thompson, *Studies from the Museum of Zoology in University College, Dundee. Vol. 1. No. 1-12* (University of Dundee 1890; reprinted 1910)

116 Mary M Paterson, *Some Memories – Mary Lily Walker of Dundee* p11

117 *History of The Grange Hotel* accessed 28/1/13 on http://www.grange-hotel.co.uk/history-grange-hotel

118 *Dundee Courier And Argus* 24th January 1889

119 ibid 25th May, 1890 & 22nd May 1891

120 DWT Papers mss44448 44449 44453, 44454 44455 44467 University of St Andrews, Special Collection

121 *Dundee Courier & Argus* July 7th 1888

122 Registration of Death doc

123 Mary M Paterson, *Some Memories – Mary Lily Walker of Dundee* p11

124 Wohl, A. S., *Octavia Hill and the Homes of the London Poor*, The Journal of British Studies, University of Chicago Press, Vol. 10, No. 2 (May, 1971), pp105–108

125 Emma Wainwright *Constructing gendered workplace 'types': The weaver-millworker distinction in Dundee's jute industry c.1880–1910* (Routledge 2010)

126 DWT Papers 44665 University of St Andrews, Special Collection

127 DWT Papers 44662 University of St Andrews, Special Collection

128 DWT Papers 44660 University of St Andrews, Special Collection

129 Elisabeth Jay, *Mrs Oliphant: 'A Fiction to Herself' – A Literary Life* (Clarendon Press Oxford 1995)

130 Ibid p143

131 DWT Papers 44656 University of St Andrews, Special Collection

132 DWT Papers 44648 University of St Andrews, Special Collection

133 From research carried out by historian Peter Kinnear

134 Mary M Paterson, *Some Memories – Mary Lily Walker of Dundee* p12

135 DWT Papers 44668 University of St Andrews, Special Collection

136 *Fifty Years Ago and Now* p10

137 DWT Papers 44673 University of St Andrews, Special Collection

138 Myra Baillie – Open Dissertation, *Mary Lily Walker of Dundee*

139 Myra Baillie – Open Dissertation, *Mary Lily Walker of Dundee*

140 Ruth D'Arcy Thomson, *D.Arcy Wentworth Thomson, The Scholar-Naturalist* (Open University Press, London 1958)

141 Myra Baillie – Open Dissertation, *Mary Lily Walker of Dundee*

142 ibid p131

143 *Dundee Advertiser*, Issue 26th October 1901

144 Gayle Davis, *The Cruel Madness of Love": Sex, Syphilis and Psychiatry in Scotland, 1880–1930* (Editions Robopi, Amsterdam 2008) p68

145 Myra Baillie – Open Dissertation, *Mary Lily Walker of Dundee*

146 Annual Report, Dundee Social Union (1900)

147 Myra Baillie – Open Dissertation, *Mary Lily Walker of Dundee*

148 Myra Baillie – Open Dissertation, *Mary Lily Walker of Dundee*

149 ibid pp91–92

150 ibid

151 Chas McKean, 'Beautifying and Improving the City: The Pursuit of Momumental Dundee during the Twentieth Century', Ed. J Tomlinson & C A Whatley, *Jute No More* (Dundee University Press 2011)

152 Myra Baillie – Open Dissertation, *Mary Lily Walker of Dundee*

153 Emma Wainwright *Constructing gendered workplace 'types': The weaver-millworker distinction in Dundee's jute industry c.1880–1910* (Routledge 2010)

154 Parliamentary Paper – Scottish Evidence, Walker Q63415/7

155 Parliamentary Paper – Scottish Evidence, Walker Q63415

156 Jose Harris, *Unemployment and Politics* (Oxford 1972) pp166–7

157 District Committee Document TC/SF/306/3, Dundee City Archives.

158 Scottish National Insurance Commission, Record SRO HH3/1

159 Mary M Paterson, *Some Memories – Mary Lily Walker of Dundee* p9

160 *Dundee Advertiser* 17th April 1912

161 Supplied by historian and researcher, David Dobson.

162 DWT Papers 44452 University of St Andrews, Special Collection

163 DWT Papers 44650 University of St Andrews, Special Collection

164 DWT Papers 44651 University of St Andrews, Special Collection

165 DWT Papers 44448 University of St Andrews, Special Collection

Chapter 6

166 Myra Baillie – Open Dissertation, *Mary Lily Walker of Dundee*

167 Ed. A W Paton & A H Millar, *British Association 1912 Dundee Handbook*

168 ibid

169 Scran UK

170 Ed. A W Paton & A H Millar, *British Association 1912 Dundee Handbook*

171 *The Times* 16th July 1915

172 Ed. A W Paton & A H Millar, *British Association 1912 Dundee Handbook*

173 ibid

174 Ed. A W Paton & A H Millar, *British Association 1912 Dundee Handbook*

175 ibid

176 Myra Baillie – Open Dissertation, *Mary Lily Walker of Dundee*

177 Tony Paterson, *Churchill: A Seat for Life* (London 1980#)

178 ibid

179 ibid

180 Tony Paterson, *Churchill: A Seat for Life* (London 1980#) p66

181 ibid

182 ibid p68

183 C A Whatley, D B. Swinfen, A M Smith, *The Life and Times of Dundee* (John Donald, Edinburgh 1993)

184 Myra Baillie – Open Dissertation, *Mary Lily Walker of Dundee*

185 Tony Paterson, *Churchill: A Seat for Life* (London 1980#) p66

186 C A Whatley, D B. Swinfen, A M Smith, *The Life and Times of Dundee* (John Donald, Edinburgh 1993)

187 W M Walker, *Juteopolis: Dundee and its Textile Workers 1885–1923* (Scottish Academic Press Edinburgh 1979) pp182–184

188 Ed. A W Paton & A H Millar, *British Association 1912 Dundee Handbook and also W M Walker, Juteopolis: Dundee and its Textile Workers 1885–1923* (Scottish Academic Press Edinburgh 1979)

Chapter 7

189 Mary M Paterson, *Some Memories – Mary Lily Walker of Dundee* p23

190 Colonial News

191 Myra Baillie – Open Dissertation, *Mary Lily Walker of Dundee*

192 Testimony of Funeral Practices in 1900 – Wm Pennycook, Perth

193 Sandeman Genealogy website

194 Mary M Paterson, *Some Memories – Mary Lily Walker of Dundee*

195 Ed. J Tomlinson & C A Whatley, *Jute No More* (Dundee University Press 2011)

196 W M Walker, *Jueoplosis: Dundee and its Textile Workers 1885–1923* (Scottish Academic Press Edinburgh 1979) pp182

197 ibid p442

198 Myra Baillie – Open Dissertation, *Mary Lily Walker of Dundee*

199 Mary M Paterson, *Some Memories – Mary Lily Walker of Dundee* p7

200 *Dundee Courier & Argus* June 22 1883

201 Mary M Paterson, *Some Memories – Mary Lily Walker of Dundee* p16

202 ibid

203 Ruth D'Arcy Thomson, *D.Arcy Wentworth Thomson, The Scholar-Naturalist* (Open University Press, London 1958)

204 Mary M Paterson, *Some Memories – Mary Lily Walker of Dundee* p16

205 Mary M Paterson, *Some Memories – Mary Lily Walker of Dundee* p8

206 Ruth D'Arcy Thomson, *D.Arcy Wentworth Thomson, The Scholar-Naturalist* (Open University Press, London 1958)

207 Ruth D'Arcy Thomson, *D.Arcy Wentworth Thomson, The Scholar-Naturalist* (Open University Press, London 1958)

208 Matthew Jarron & Cathy Caudwell, *D'Arcy Thomson and his Zoology Museum in Dundee* (UoD Museum Services 2010)

209 ibid

210 *Dundee Postal Directory 1912*

211 DWT Papers 44449 University of St Andrews, Special Collection

212 DWT Papers 44453, University of St Andrews, Special Collection

213 DWT Papers 44454, University of St Andrews, Special Collection

214 DWT Papers 44455, University of St Andrews, Special Collection

215 From research by David Dobson

216 DWT Papers 44467 University of St Andrews, Special Collection

217 DWT Papers 44456, University of St Andrews, Special Collection

218 DWT Papers 44457, University of St Andrews, Special Collection

219 Matthew Jarron & Cathy Caudwell, *D'Arcy Thomson and his Zoology Museum in Dundee* (UoD Museum Services 2010)

220 Ruth D'Arcy Thomson, *D.Arcy Wentworth Thomson, The Scholar-Naturalist* (Open University Press, London 1958)

221 Myra Baillie – Open Dissertation, *Mary Lily Walker of Dundee*

222 Peter Kinnear

223 ibid

224 Scotsman Obituaries

225 Mary M Paterson, *Some Memories – Mary Lily Walker of Dundee* p14

226 ibid

227 *Dundee Courier* 3rd July 1913

228 Photograph shown in *The Courier*, Dated 4th July 1913

229 DWT Papers ms44685 University of St Andrews, Special Collection

230 DWT Papers ms44689 University of St Andrews, Special Collection

231 Mary M Paterson, *Some Memories – Mary Lily Walker of Dundee*

Chapter 8

232 DWT Papers ms44689 University of St Andrews, Special Collection

233 Scottish Government Publications, 2009, *Early Years Framework*

234 ibid

235 Dundee Valuation Roll (Dundee City Archives)

Index

222